EVERGREEN FORM STUDIES

DESIGN CHARACTERISTICS of CONIFERS

compiled and collected by

Gary O. Robinette

drawings by

Susan Van Gieson

VNR VAN NOSTRAND REINHOLD COMPANY
NEW YORK   CINCINNATI   TORONTO   LONDON   MELBOURNE

Copyright © 1983 by Van Nostrand Reinhold Company Inc.

Library of Congress Catalog Card Number: 83-1237
ISBN: 0-442-22337-4

Manufactured in the United States of America

Published by Van Nostrand Reinhold Company Inc.
135 West 50th Street, New York, N.Y. 10020

Van Nostrand Reinhold Publishing
1410 Birchmount Road
Scarborough, Ontario M1P 2E7, Canada

Van Nostrand Reinhold
480 Latrobe Street
Melbourne, Victoria 3000, Australia

Van Nostrand Reinhold Company Limited
Molly Millars Lane
Wokingham, Berkshire, England

15 14 13 12 11 10 9 8 7 6 5 4 3 2 1

Library of Congress Cataloging in Publication Data

Robinette, Gary O.
    Evergreen form studies.

    Bibliography: p.
    1. Ornamental conifers — North America. 2. Landscape
architecture — Designs and plans. I. Van Gieson, Susan.
II. Title. III. Title: Design characteristics of
conifers.
SB428.V36   1983   715′.2   83-1237
ISBN 0-442-22337-4

contents

Introduction

This is a specialized book which fills the gap left by other books. This book was originally designed for people in the landscape industry and is for use by people who draw plants and who use plants for design purposes. It is not designed for foresters, growers or botanists. It is not an introductory book. It is a book for someone who already knows something about the plants. There are plenty of other books which deal with the buds, the twigs, growth rates, diseases, and geographic ranges, and which give a verbal description of each of the plants. Most of these other books are covered in the bibliographic references mentioned in the back of this book.

This book deals with the most commonly used coniferous evergreens. It deals with those grown in all geographic regions of North America. It is designed for people who draw or specify plants, or for people who place buildings or activities among existing plants. The purpose of this book is to show, in elevational form, the typical coniferous evergreens in their normal landscape size and shape. It does not show the largest, the smallest, or the most picturesque of each of these plants. It shows the most typical shape of each of these plants when found or used in a landscape setting. Some plants are shown in more than one form and some are shown in both the immature and mature forms. Individual plants when grown in an open setting without competition from other plants will obviously take a different shape or form than when the same plant is grown in a forest setting in competition with a large number of other plants. Also, many plants are very similar when young, but when they grow older, they take on the characteristic form or shape of their particular species. This should be kept in mind by the landscape designer when specifying these plants.

In this book each of the coniferous evergreens are shown in three forms. They are shown in an outline form as they would appear normally as they reach maturity. They are also shown in a rendered or delineated form which indicates the texture, the character or the quality of the individual plant type. They are also shown in reduced silhouettes, in a group or family, for a comparison of the relative size, shape or character of any individual plant. There are a great number of ways that the drawings in this particular book can be used by landscape architects, landscape nurserymen, architects, engineers, planners or landscape designers. Some of these are suggested in the following introductory section of the book.

Generally these forms and shapes have been adapted from photographs and drawings and a great number of other sources. This collection is not a complete overview of all of the coniferous evergreen types which are used in all sections of North America, but they do suggest those most commonly used in landscape settings or situations or which are most commonly sold by wholesale and retail nurserymen. Hopefully this first collection of coniferous evergreen plant form drawings, which is done at the same scale, will be of use and benefit to a wide audience in years to come.

how to use this book

Most landscape designers, landscape nurserymen and landscape architects who use plant materials learn to identify coniferous evergreen trees and shrubs by referring to the buds, needles and cones or seeds of the tree at different stages of growth and development. To know what a tree is when you see it is of some importance. However, to a landscape designer that is not nearly as important as it is to be able to communicate to others the ultimate form, shape, size, character and texture of the mature plant. To specify or place a precise plant in a specific location on a landscape plan requires an understanding and a knowledge of the ultimate form and shape of the plant at maturity. Any cursory review of a typical developed or planned landscape will show numerous instances where plants have grown too large, spread too far, or are too tall for the situation in which they have been placed. They probably were of an appropriate size when they were planted, or possibly even midway through their growth cycle, but as they mature and become too large they are many times inappropriate for a specific location.

This book is not an identification book for the various coniferous evergreens. This book is designed to help you as a landscape designer communicate and to help you design more effectively and intelligently. There are already a great many books which tell you in great detail of the buds, the needles, the lumber potential, the size of the cones and the geographic range of the various coniferous landscape plants. Many of these have been developed for foresters or for botanists. This book has been developed for landscape designers to assist you in a comparison of the form, texture, height and spread at maturity of the most commonly used evergreen landscape plants. This book has been designed to provide you assistance in drawing, depiction and delineation of these landscape plants in elevational or sectional views. This book contains a comparison of the ultimate form of one plant or one group of plants to another.

The drawings of the coniferous evergreens in this book do not represent the largest nor the smallest of a particular species. The drawings do not represent a specific tree, but each drawing is a generalized representation of characteristics of a given tree, shrub or ground cover plant. This drawing indicates the forms generally seen in a healthy, well-maintained landscape plant. Obviously, some trees grow from 200-300 feet at maturity. Obviously it is not possible within the scale limitations of the pages of this particular book to show plants at that scale and at the same time to show some of the smaller spreading evergreens. The drawings in this book illustrate the form of these evergreen plants when grown in the open, rather than in crowded conditions. Basically these drawings indicate what can usually be expected in these plants in their predictable ultimate form as they reach maturity. Obviously considerable variation may occur in the form of trees or shrubs which are growing in cities or crowded conditions, such as in large forests or groves.

The following suggestions are offered to assist you in making maximum use of this book and to save you time and money in drawing some of the typical coniferous landscape plants which you normally use in each of the geographic regions in North America. All of, the plants in this book are drawn at 1/8 scale (1/8″ = 1′ 0″). That is, the plants are drawn at a scale whereby 1″ equals 8′ of the ultimate plant size. Therefore it is possible to reduce or enlarge these plant form drawings in order to use them at any scale. A 1/2 reduction of the plant would represent a 1/16 scale (1/16″ = 1′ 0″), whereas a four times reduction would show the plant at 32nd scale (1/32″ = 1′ 0″). It is also possible to reduce these plants for use on metric or engineering scale drawings. This reduction can be done manually, or by using a reduction machine or copier. The reduction may also be done using a photostat camera or photographic equipment.

At the same time it is also possible to enlarge these drawings to 1/4″ scale, 1/2″ scale or at a scale where 1″ = 1′.
The scale and character of the plant form drawings in this book can be changed by enlarging or reducing the drawings. In this way the basic form drawings are able to be used in many different types of presentation or communication.

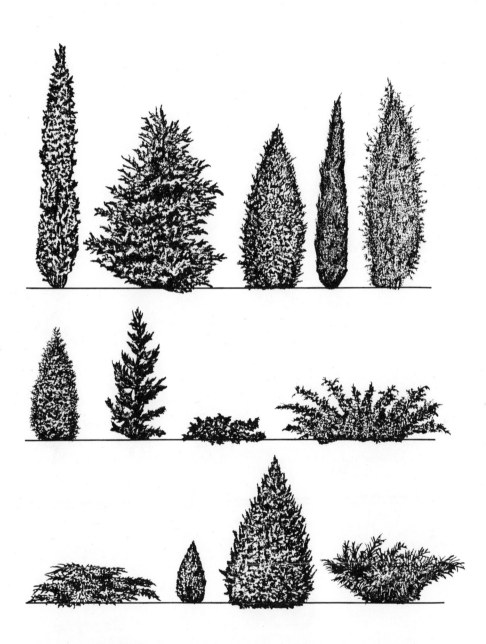

It is possible to use the drawings in this book to quickly and easily show clients or customers the variations between different species in the same family. The form, shape and texture of the various junipers can be shown at the same scale for easier communication and comparison.

It is also possible to reduce or enlarge a portion of the plant, to use it as a foreground or a background for a perspective drawing. By just drawing the appropriate architecture you can show in elevation or section how the proposed planting would appear around the building This could be used by a nursery salesman, a landscape architect, or planners wishing to illustrate the relative size and shape of potential plants to be used in various situations.

Many types of pine are very similar in form when they are young and immature. This is confusing to many designers and to purchasers of plants since they all appear to be interchangeable in form.

However as the different types of pines grow and mature they assume much more different and distinctive shapes. Everyone using these conifers needs to be aware of not only the ultimate size but the eventual form they may be expected to take.

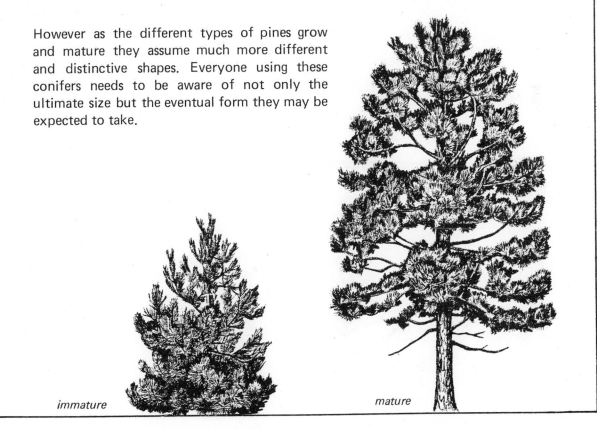

immature

mature

mature

immature

mature

immature

The drawings in this book enable you to see and to show more easily and quickly the eventual form of different types of pines as they grow and mature.

immature

mature

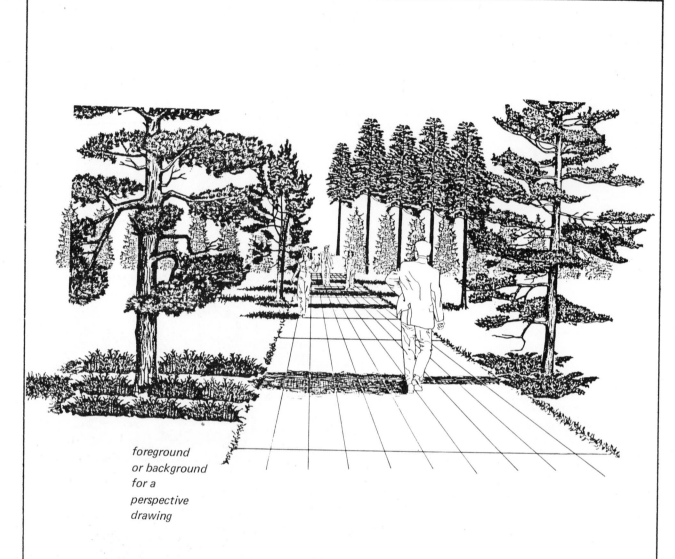

foreground
or background
for a
perspective
drawing

You can also enlarge, reduce or lighten and darken the drawings using the plant forms to help create a very quick perspective drawing showing proposed plants as they would appear at maturity.

It is possible to enlarge or reduce even the outline drawings and not only the plants but also to use them in abstract designs or as design elements. The drawings can also be copied on film and thus superimposed on to one another.

*combine with
other plants*

    Some evergreens are able to grow and survive in many different climatic regions. Using these drawings it is possible to show how those conifers might appear when they are used with the indigenous plants of each of those regions. Since this book contains drawings of many of the conifers which grow in the various regions of North America, it is possible to show the plants as they can be combined or used together with other plants which grow in different climatic situations.

By combining the coniferous plant form drawings in this book with drawings of other plant types it is possible to show how a particular planting would look in different climatic or geographic regions.

combine with other plants

By adding scale drawings of people, cars and street furniture you can show how an area would look when the plants mature.

It is possible to combine the drawings in this book with other drawings of deciduous plants to show how a specific area would look in both winter without leaves or needles and in summer when all of the plants are in full leaf. This is valuable not only for design studies but for illustration to a client or to other design professionals.

winter

summer

Some species of conifers take on very distinctive shapes depending on where they are grown and the culture they receive. The Monterey Cypress, for instance, can be a very formal pyramid, an oval as it matures or it may assume the very dramatic and picturesque form so often seen in posters, photographs or post-cards. This can be seen and shown using these drawings.

The drawings can also be used as models for plants to be drawn in perspective sketches, or as a basis for renderings or sketches of individual plants or groups of plants. This delineation or rendering may be done in pen and ink, pencil, felt tip pen, charcoal or on coquille board. It is also possible to reproduce these drawings on dry transfer sheets by a variety of processes at a number of scales for use repetitively in the private professional office or in a government agency.

pen and ink

pencil

pen and ink

ball point pen

charcoal

charcoal

felt tip pen

It is also possible to digitize or convert to numbers the plant forms contained in this publication and to convert them to a form which could be made available on a computer printout or reproduced by a digital plotter. In this way, it would be possible to utilize the computer plotter as a drafting tool to assist in building libraries of the plant forms for a specific geographic region or area.

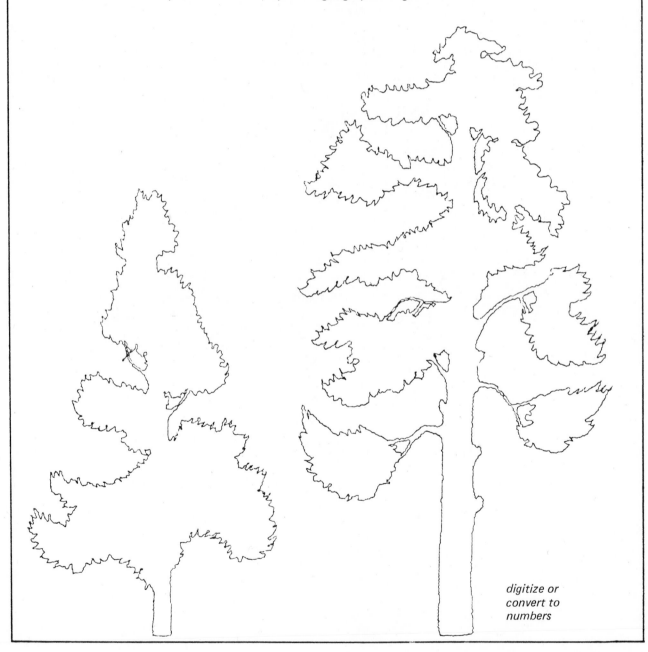

digitize or convert to numbers

These are just a few of the ways the material in this book could be utilized. Hopefully, it will be of use to you and will assist you in achieving effective environmental design more quickly, more effectively and completely and at a reduced cost in both time and money.

The ultimate plant form is an important design consideration in the use of any landscape plants. Many of the coniferous evergreens change so dramatically from their small, immature form to the ultimate mature form grown in a landscape setting. It is important for all landscape designers to know and understand them and then to show those specific and particular differences. This book has been designed to help you do just that.

EVERGREEN FORM STUDIES

DESIGN CHARACTERISTICS of CONIFERS

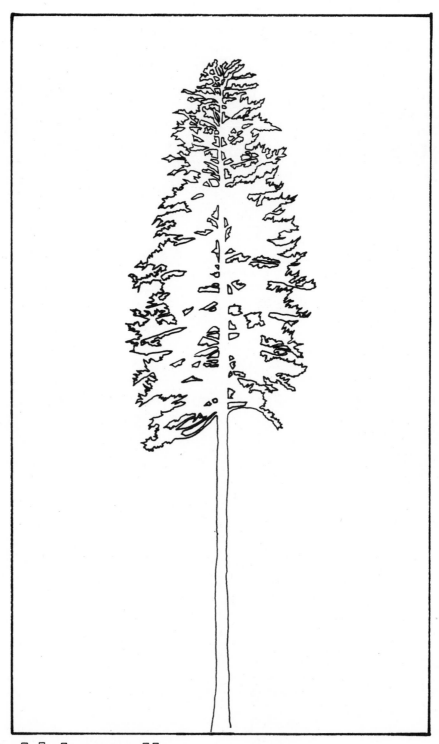

Abies alba

Abies alba

Abies amabilis

Abies amabilis

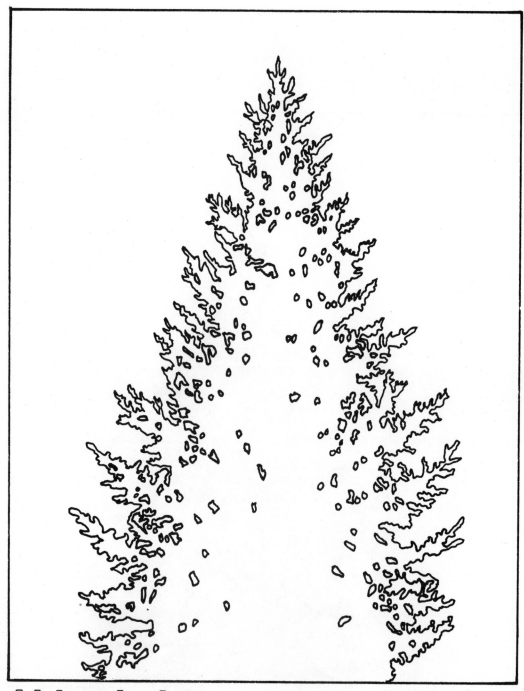

Abies balsamae

Abies balsamae

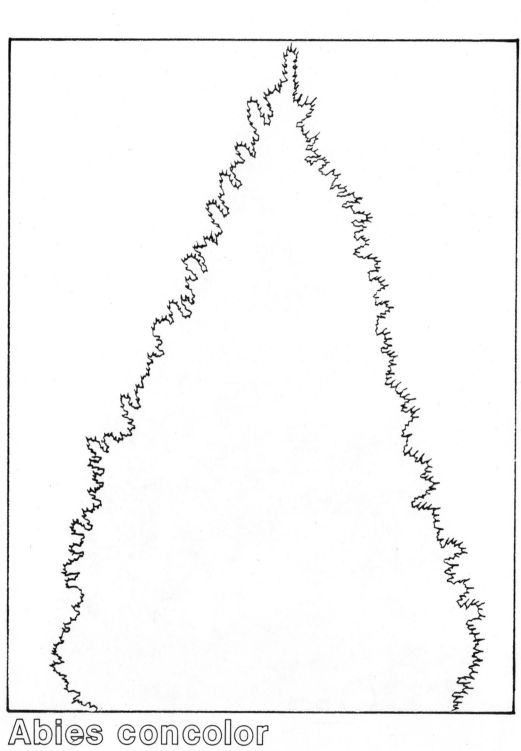

Abies concolor

Abies concolor

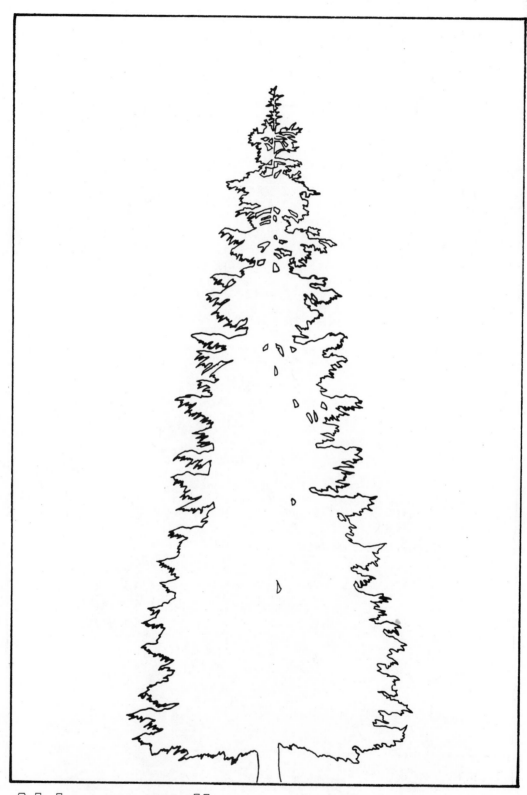

Abies grandis

Abies grandis

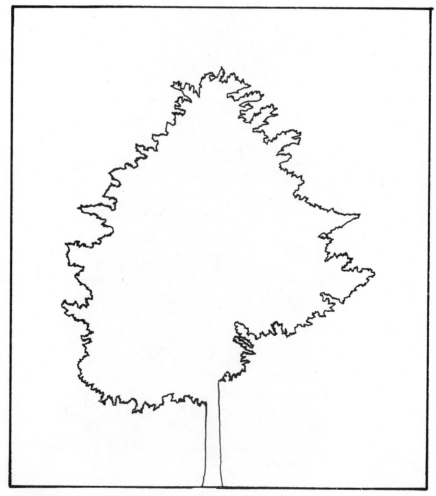

Abies koreana

Abies koreana

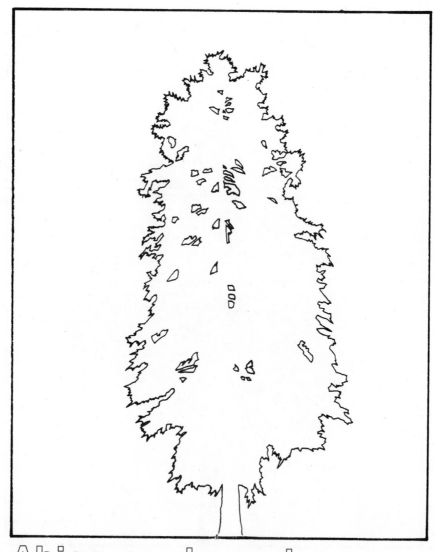

Abies nordmanniana

Abies nordmanniana

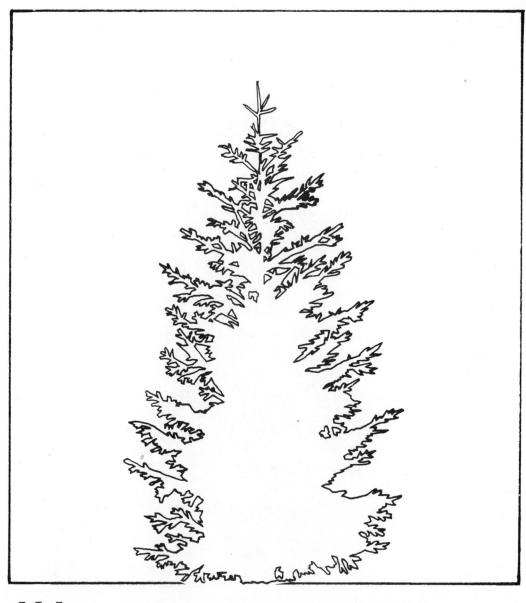

Abies procera

Abies procera

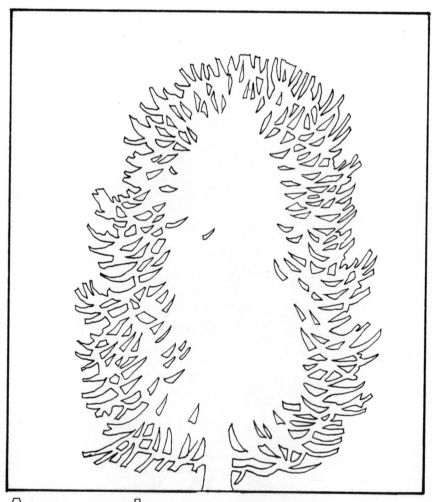

Araucaria araucana

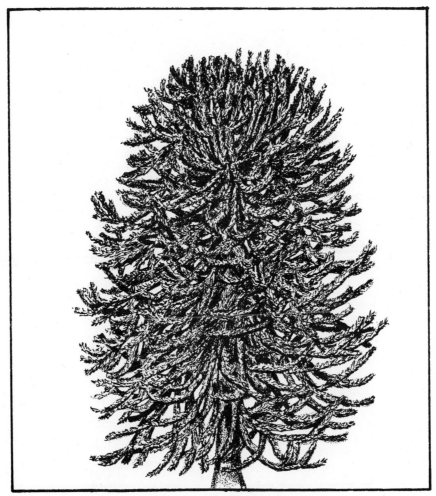

Araucaria araucana

Araucaria araucana

Araucaria araucana

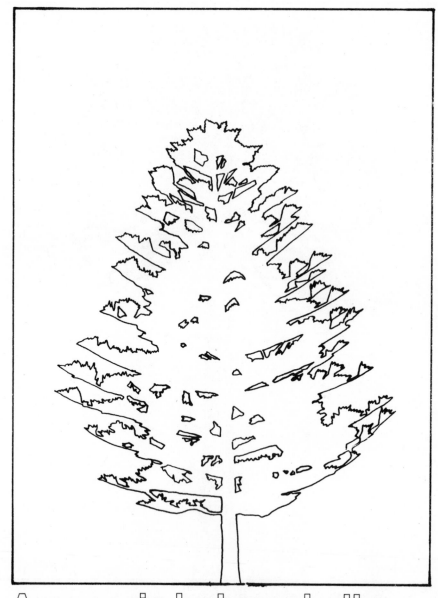

Araucaria heterophylla

Araucaria heterophylla

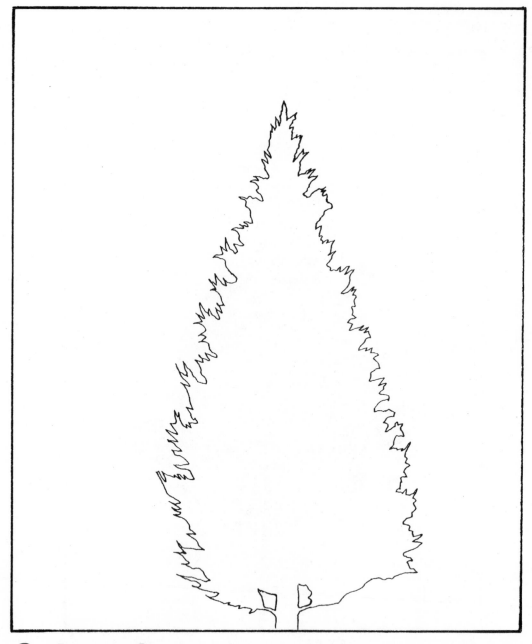

Calocedrus decurrens

Calocedrus decurrens

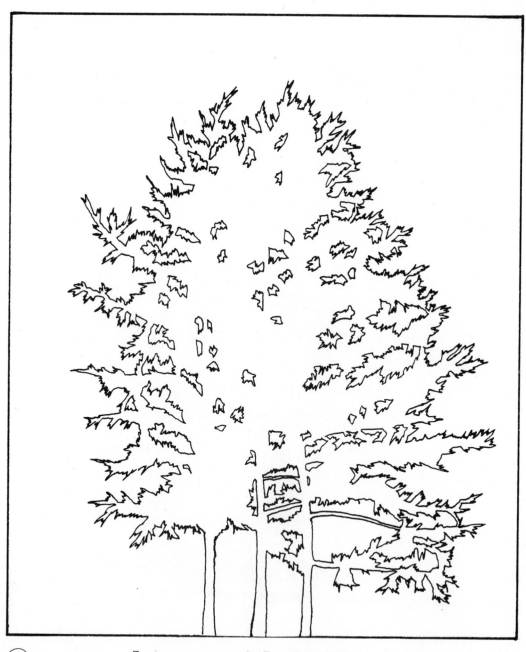

Casuarina equisitifolia

Casuarina equisitifolia

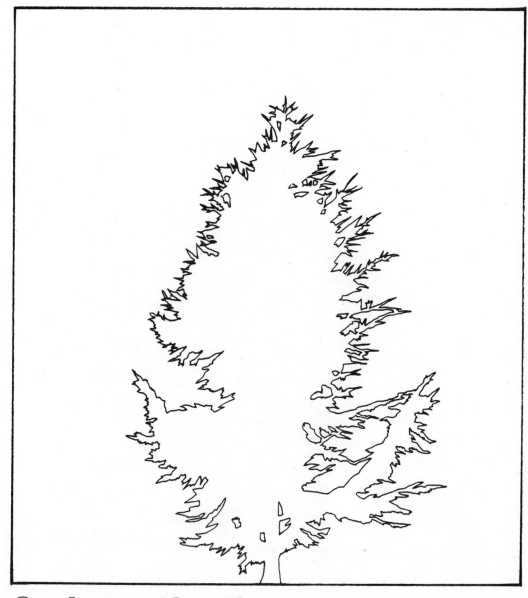

Cedrus atlantica

Cedrus atlantica

Cedrus deodora

Cedrus deodora

Cedrus libani

Cedrus libani

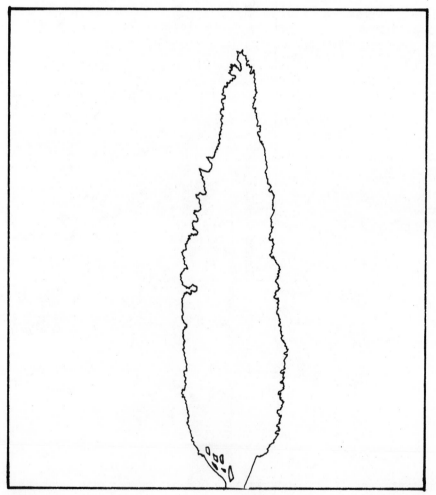

Chamaecyparis lawsoniana

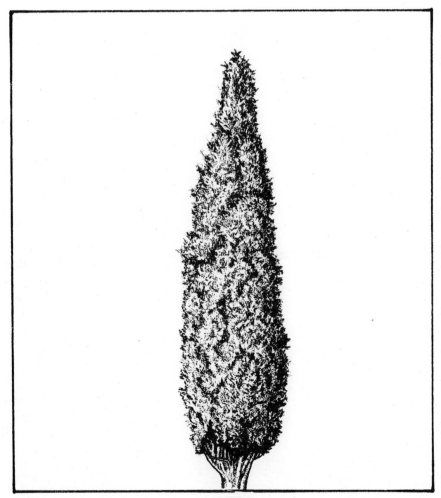

Chamaecyparis lawsoniana

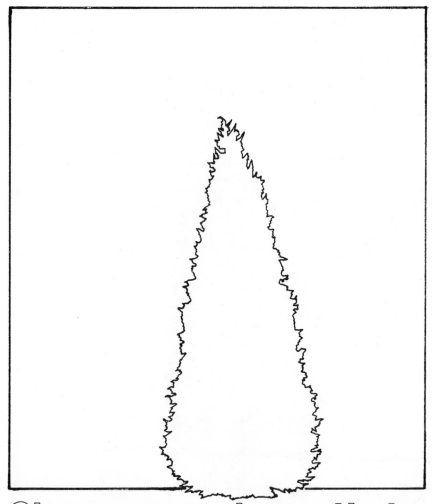

Chamaecyparis nootkatensis

Chamaecyparis nootkatensis

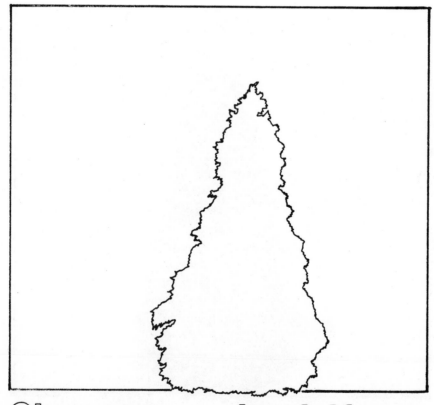

Chamaecyparis pisifera

Chamaecyparis pisifera

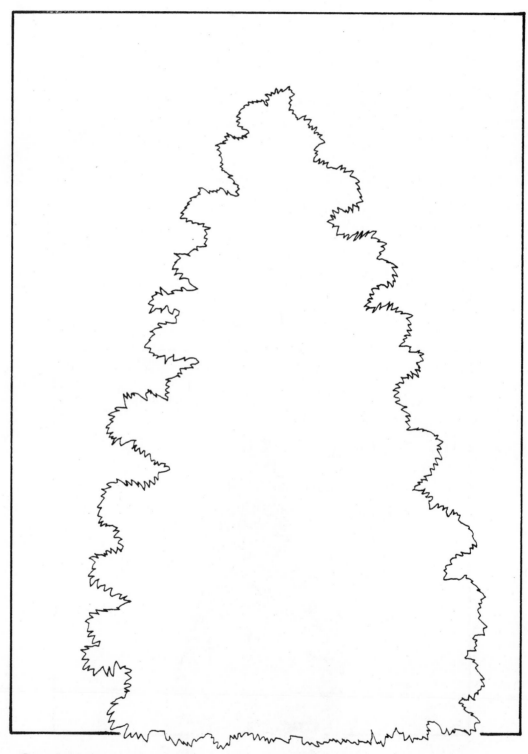

Cryptomeria japonica

Cryptomeria japonica

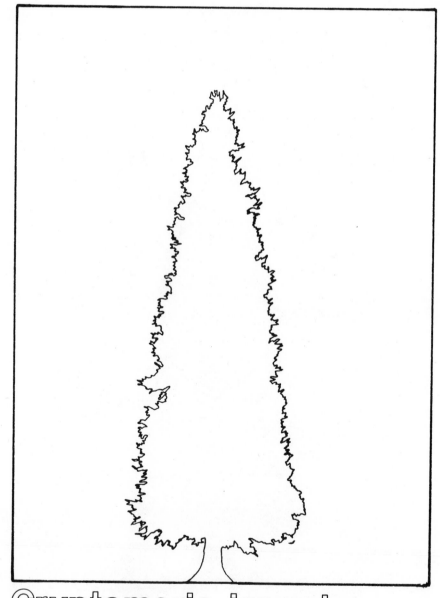

Cryptomeria japonica

Cryptomeria japonica

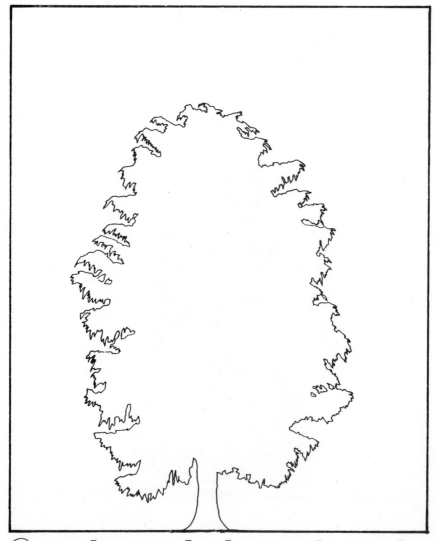

Cryptomeria japonica elegans

Cryptomeria japonica elegans

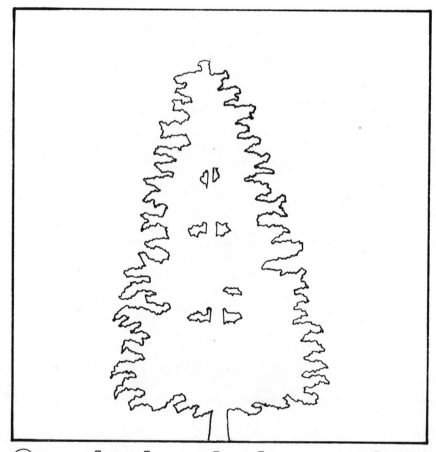

Cunninghamia lanceolota

Cunninghamia lanceolota

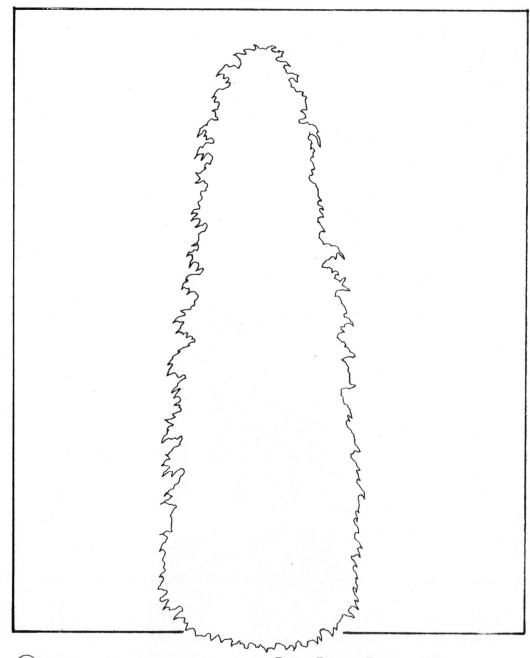

Cupressocyparis leylandi

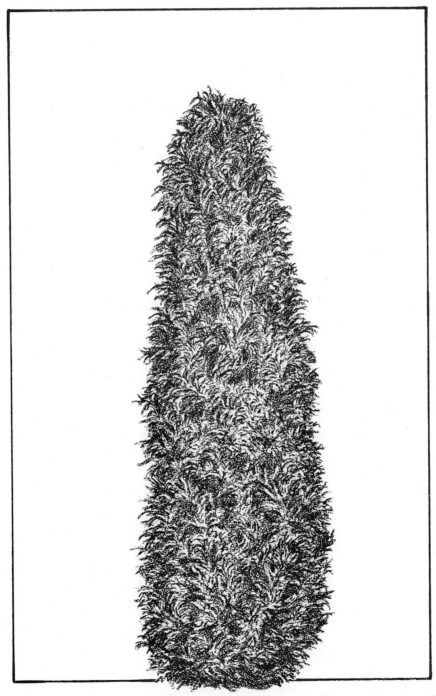

Cupressocyparis leylandi

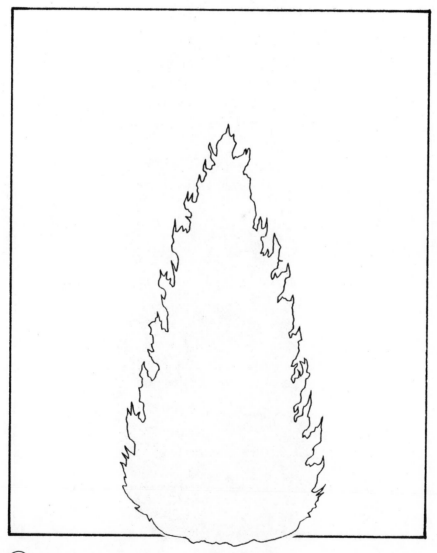

Cupressus glabra

Cupressus glabra

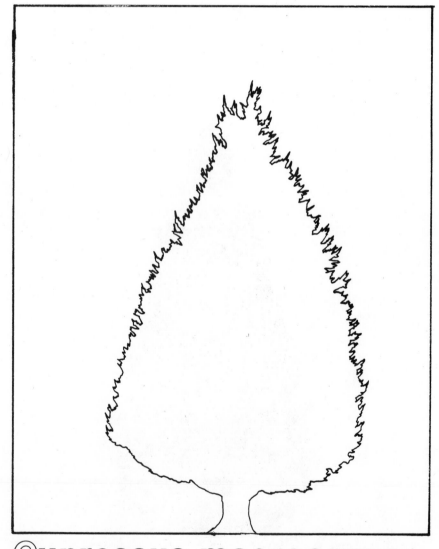

Cupressus macrocarpa

Cupressus macrocarpa

Cupressus macrocarpa

Cupressus macrocarpa

Cupressus macrocarpa

Cupressus macrocarpa

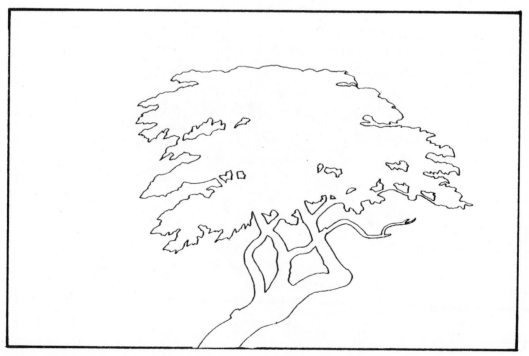

Cupressus macrocarpa

Cupressus macrocarpa

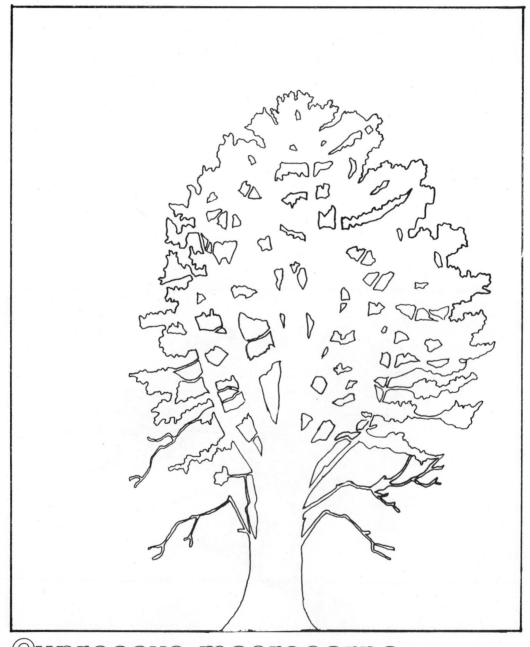

Cupressus macrocarpa

Cupressus macrocarpa

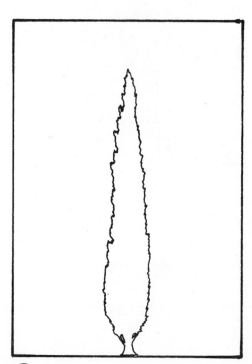 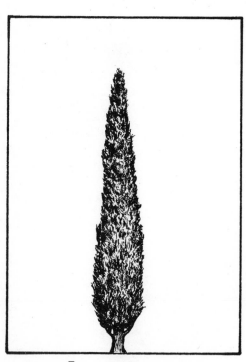

Cupressus sempervirens
`Columnar´

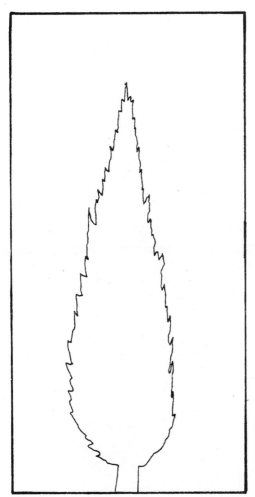 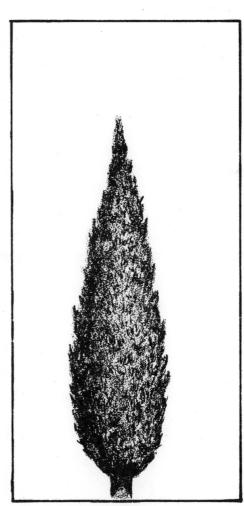

Cupressus sempervirens
`Columnar´

63

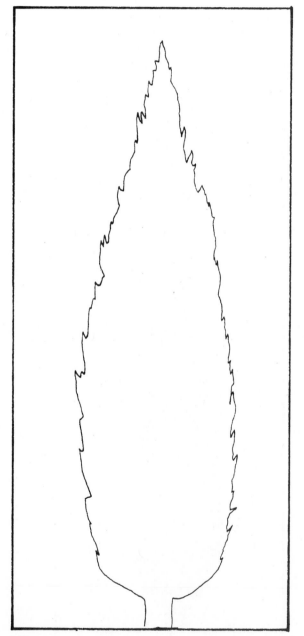 

Cupressus semervirens `Columnar´

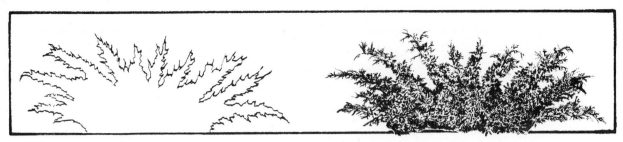

Juniperus chinenis `Hetzi´

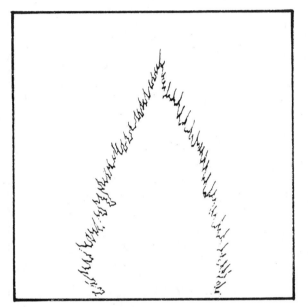

Juniperus chinensis `Ketleeri´

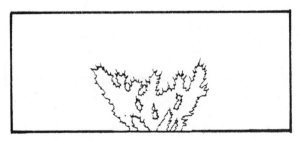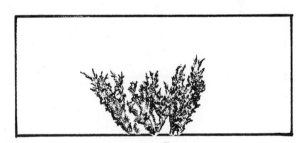

Juniperus chinensis `Maneyi´

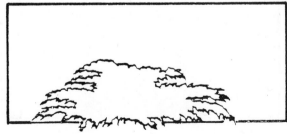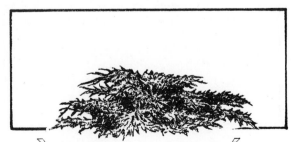

Juniperus chinensis `Pfitzeriana´

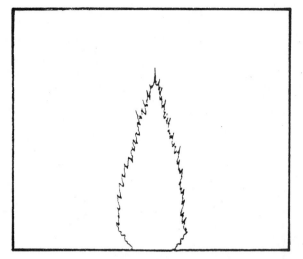

Juniperus chinensis pyramidalis

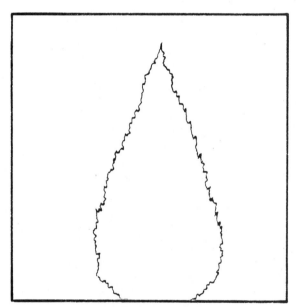

Juniperus chinensis pyramidalis

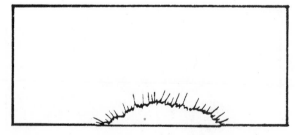

Juniperus chinensis `Sargenti´

 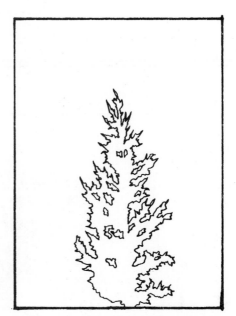

Juniperus chinensis torulosa

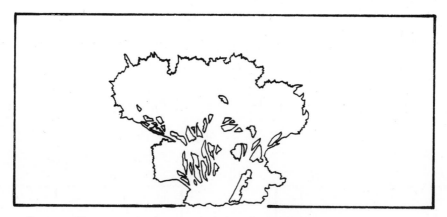

Juniperus communis

Juniperus communis

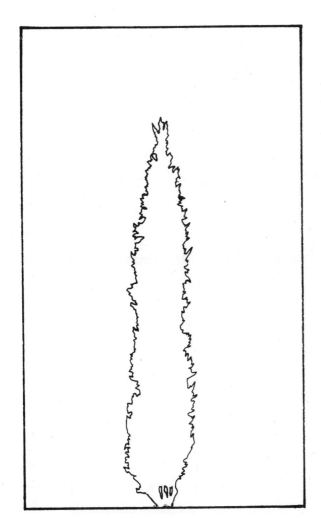 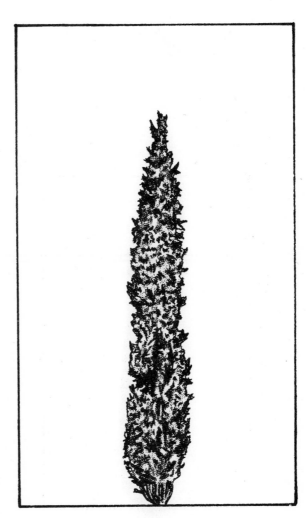

Juniperus communis

69

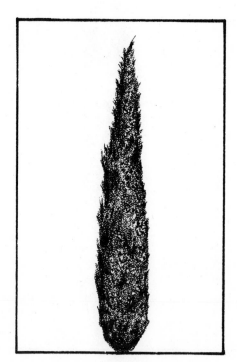 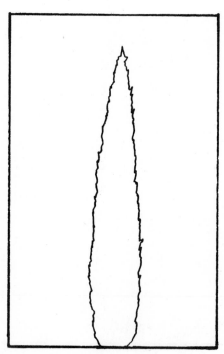

Juniperus communis `Hibernica´

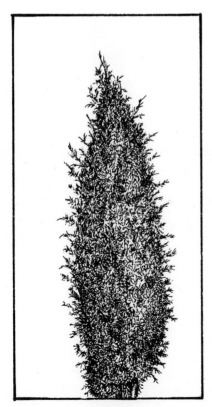 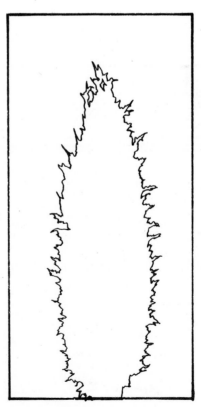

Juniperus communis `Suecica´

71

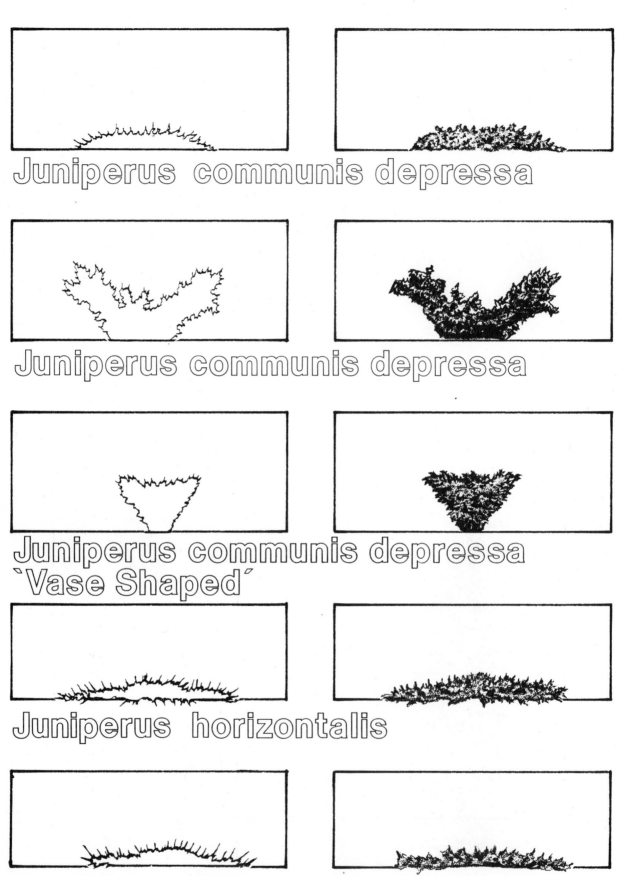

Juniperus communis depressa

Juniperus communis depressa

Juniperus communis depressa
`Vase Shaped´

Juniperus horizontalis

Juniperus horizontalis `Bar Harbor´

Juniperus horizontalis `Douglasi´

Juniperus horizontalis `Plumosa´

Juniperus horizontalis `Wiltoni´

Juniperus procumbens

Juniperus deppeana pachyphloes

Juniperus deppeana pachyphlaea

75

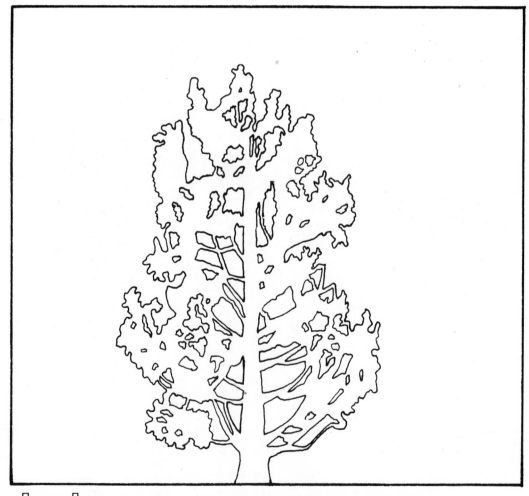

Juniperus monosperma

Juniperus monosperma

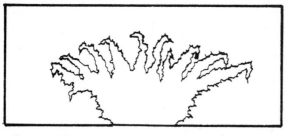 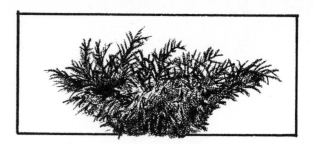

Juniperus sabina

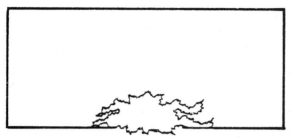 

Juniperus sabina tamariscifolia

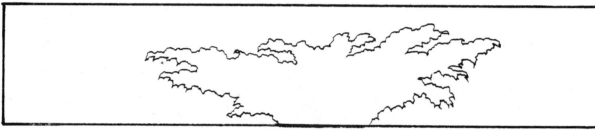

Juniperus sabina `Vonehron´

Juniperus sabina `Vonehron´

Juniperus squmata `Meyeri´

Juniperus scopulorum

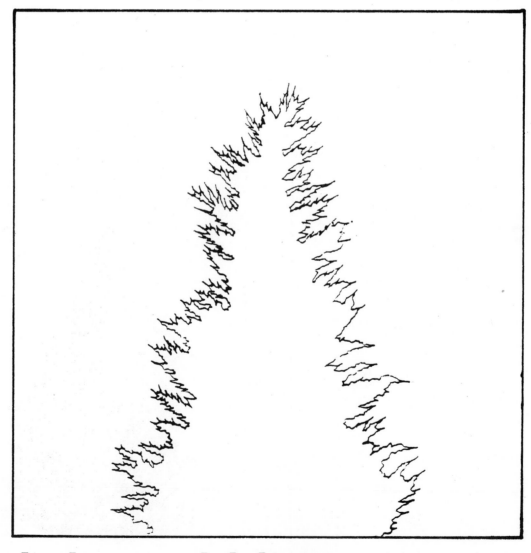

Juniperus viginiana

Juniperus virginiana

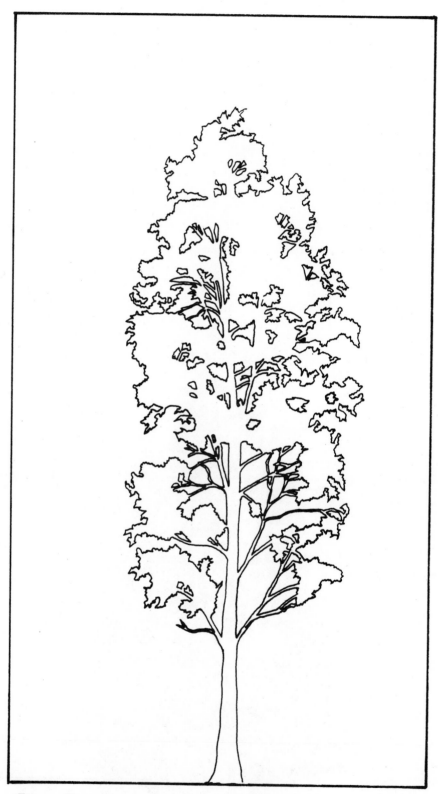

Juniperus viginiana

Juniperus viginiana

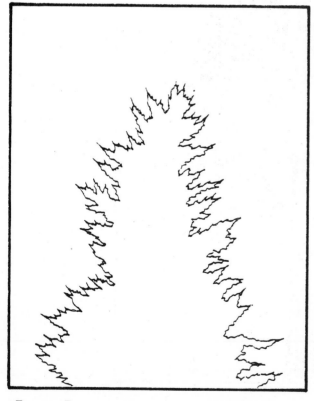 

Juniperus virginiana `Canaerti´

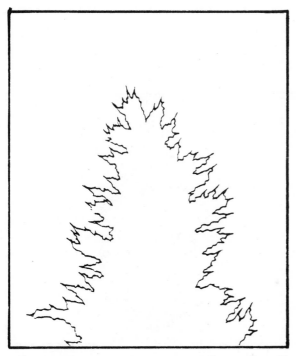 

Juniperus virginiana `Glauca`

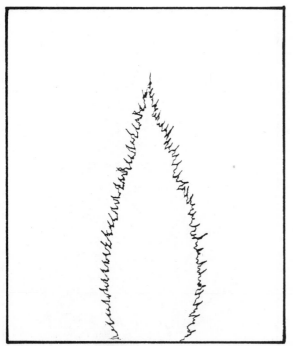

Juniperus virginiana `Hilli´

Larix decidua

Larix decidua

Larix decidua

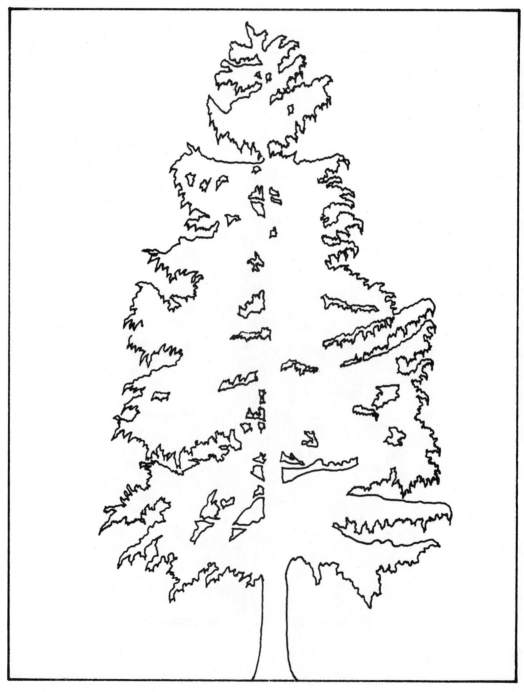

Larix larcina

Larix laricina

Larix laricina

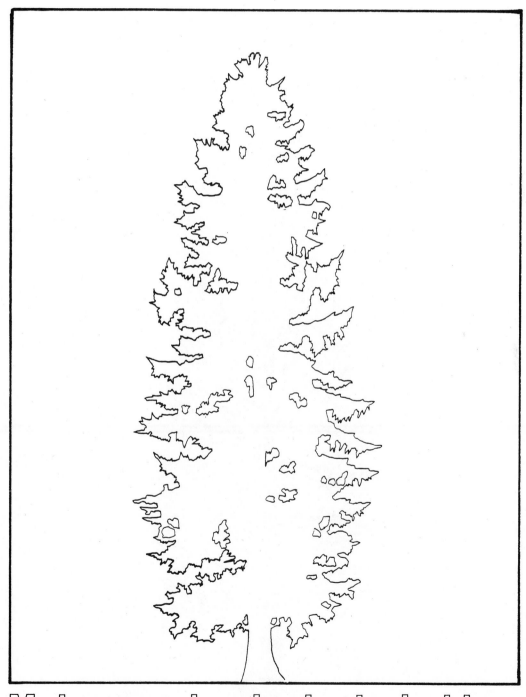

Metasequoia glyptostroboides

Metasequoia glyptostroboides

Metasequoia glyptostroboides

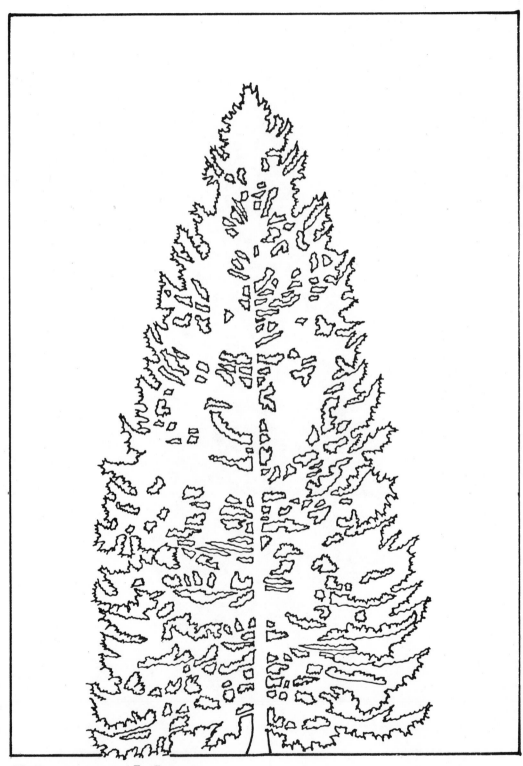

Picea abies

Picea abies

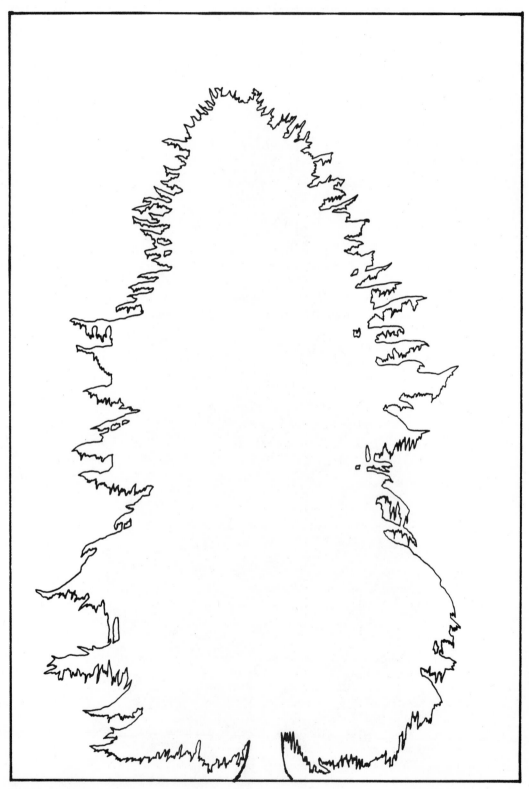

Picea breweriana

Picea breweriana

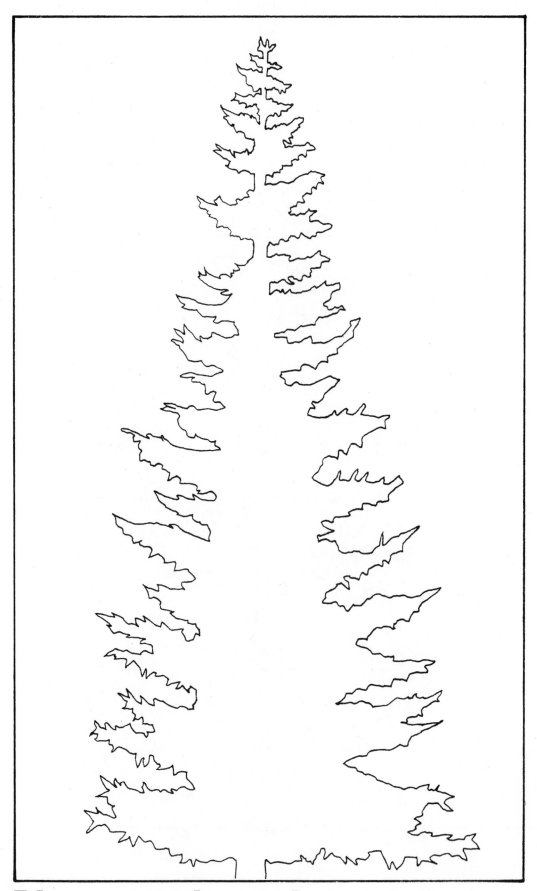

Picea engelmanni

Picea engelmanni

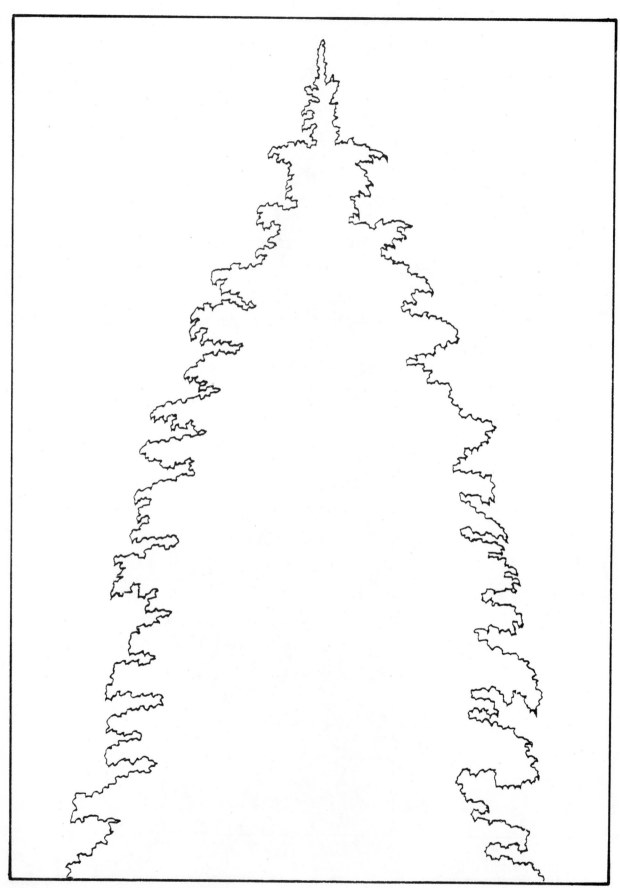

Picea glauca

Picea glauca

103

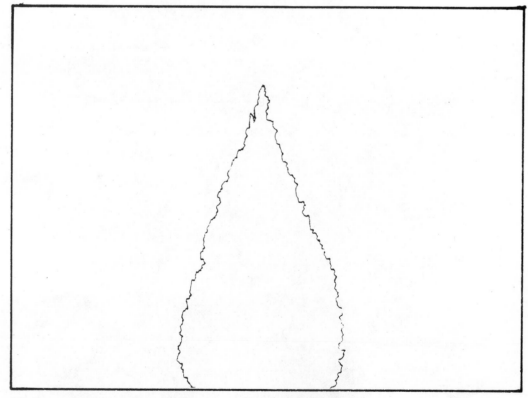

Picea glauca densata

Picea glauca densata

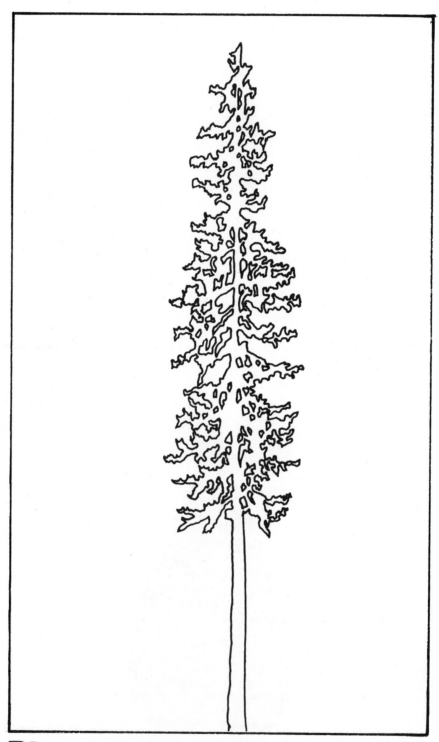

Picea mariana

Picea mariana

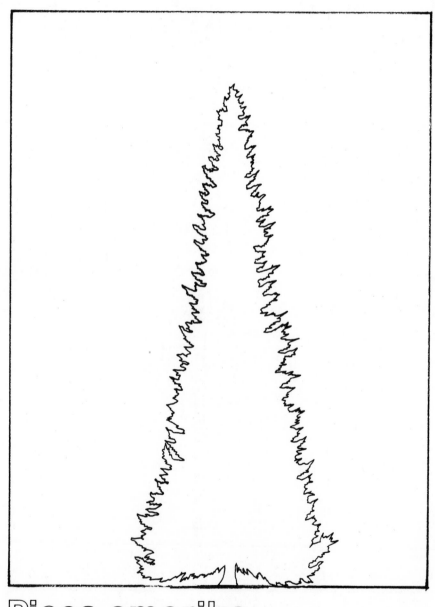

Picea omorika

Picea omorika

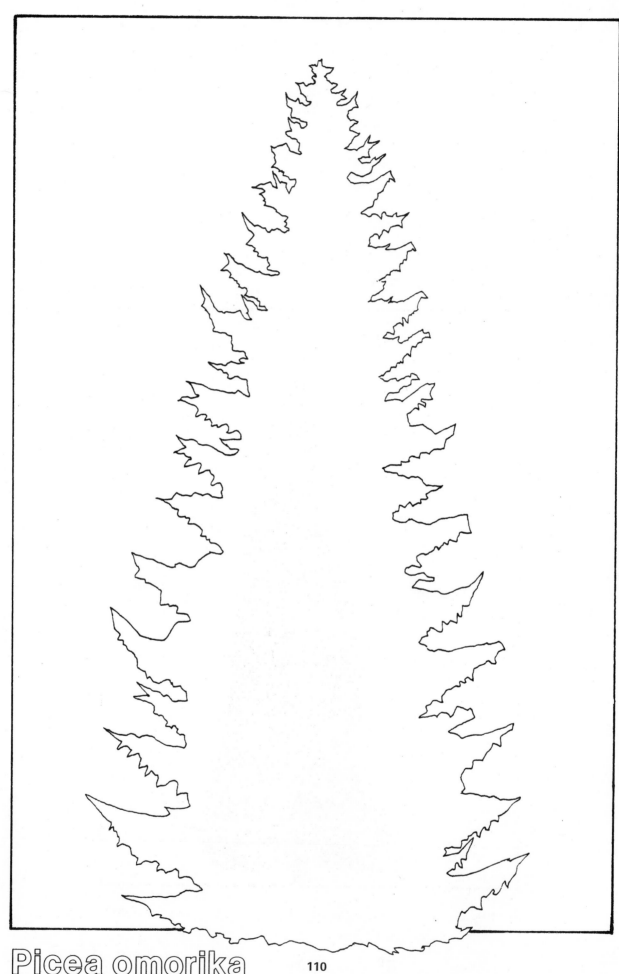

Picea omorika

110

Picea omorika

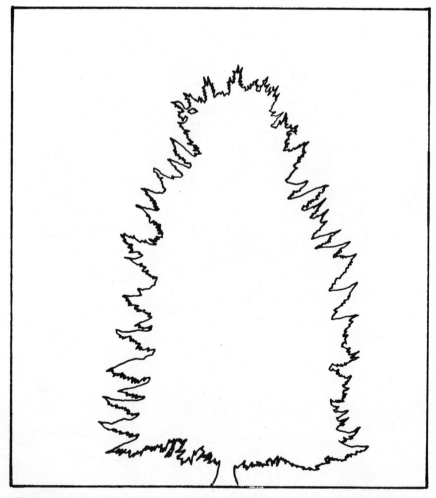

Picea orientalis

Picea orientalis

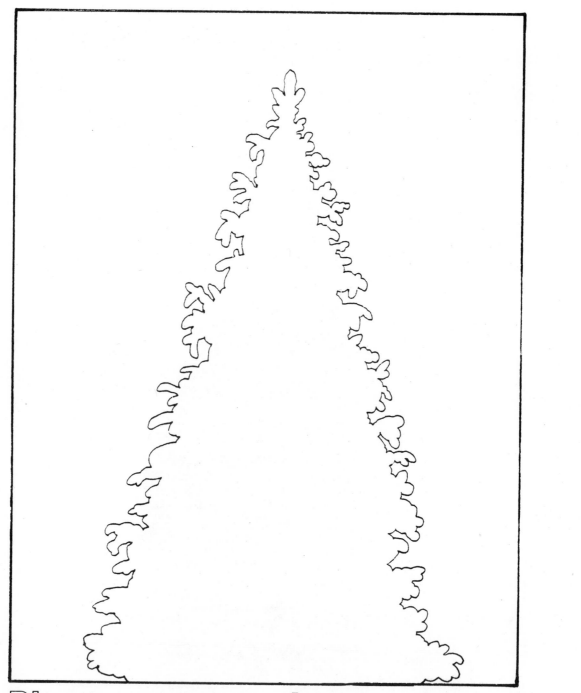

Picea pungens glauca

Picea pungens glauca

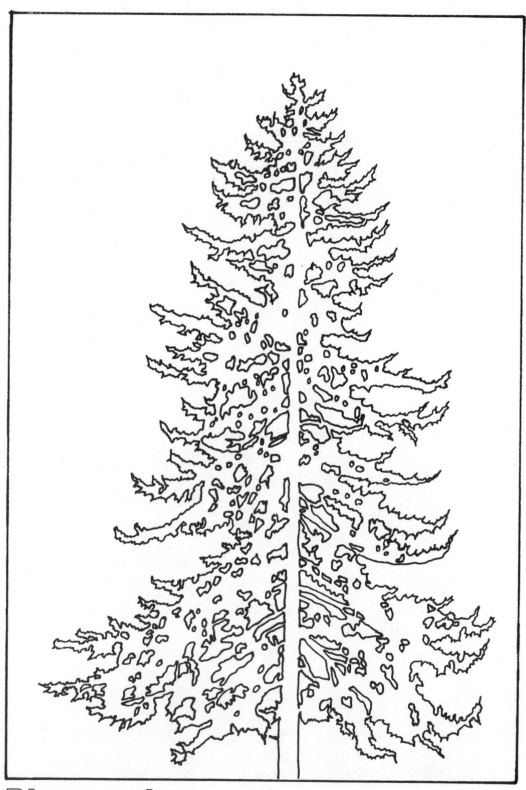

Picea rubra

Picea rubra

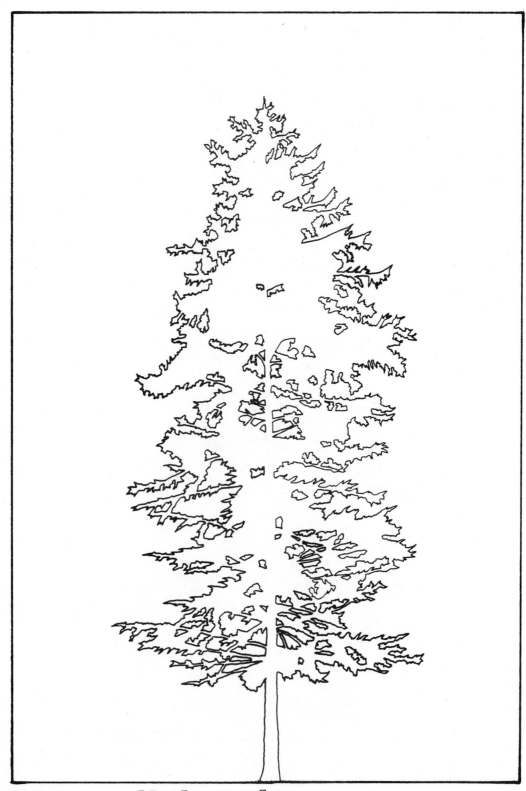

Picea sitchensis

Picea sitchensis

Pinus albicaulis

Pinus albicaulis

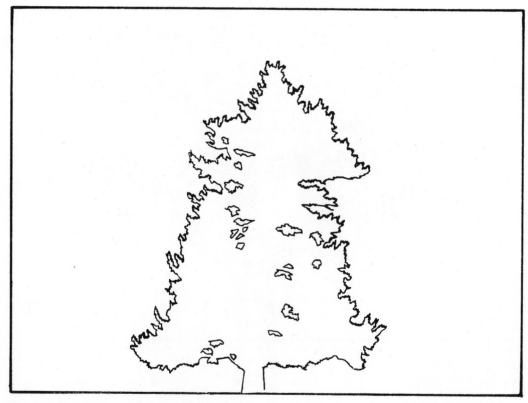

Pinus aristata

Pinus aristata

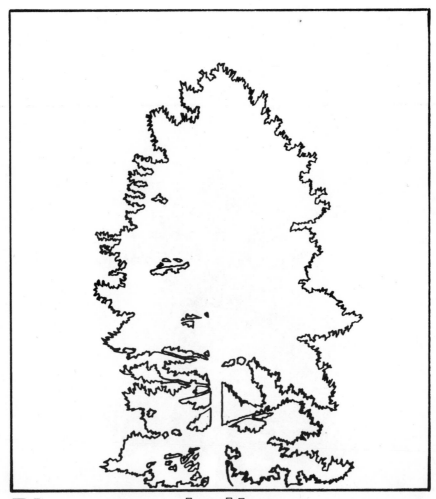

Pinus ayachuite

Pinus ayachuite

Pinus balfouriana

Pinus balfouriana

Pinus banksiana

Pinus banksiana

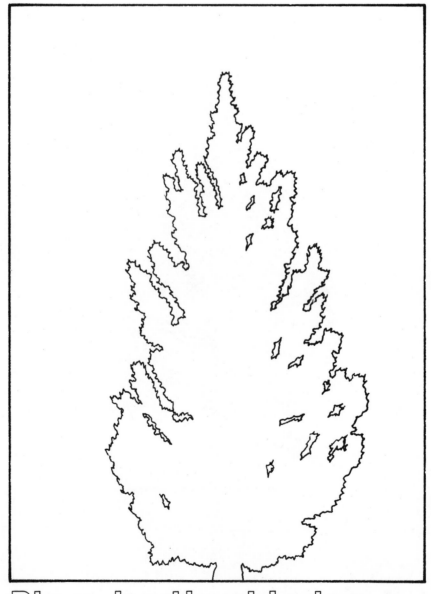

Pinus brutia eldarica

Pinus brutia eldarica

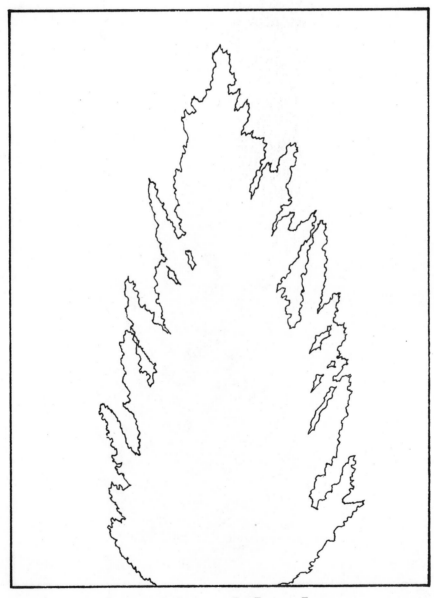

Pinus brutia eldarica

Pinus brutia eldarica

133

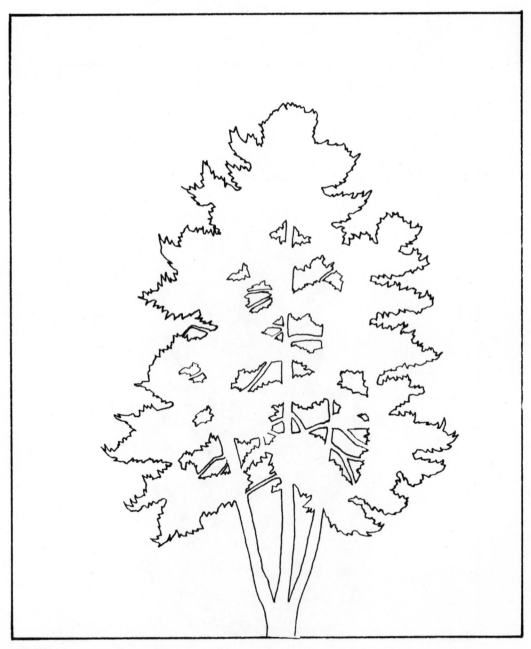

Pinus bungeana

Pinus bungeana

Pinus canariensis

Pinus canariensis

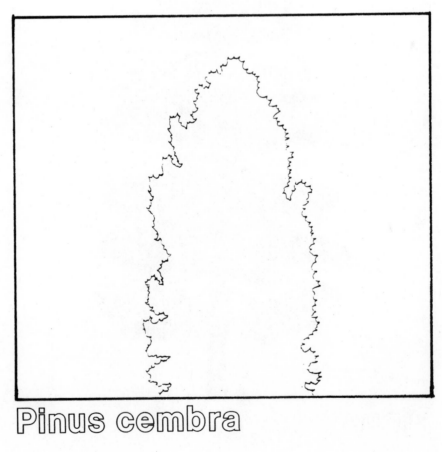

Pinus cembra

Pinus cembra

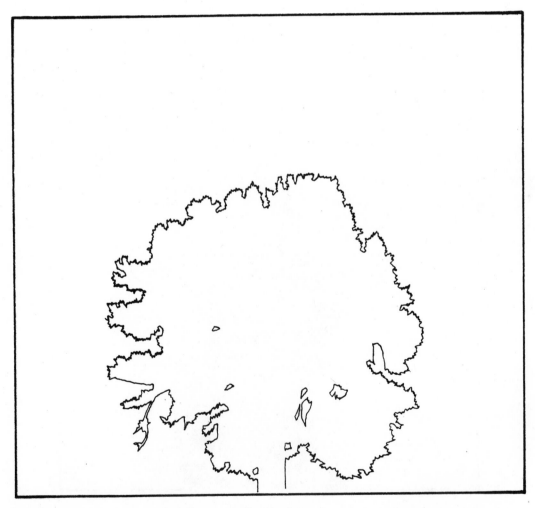

Pinus cembroides

Pinus cembroides

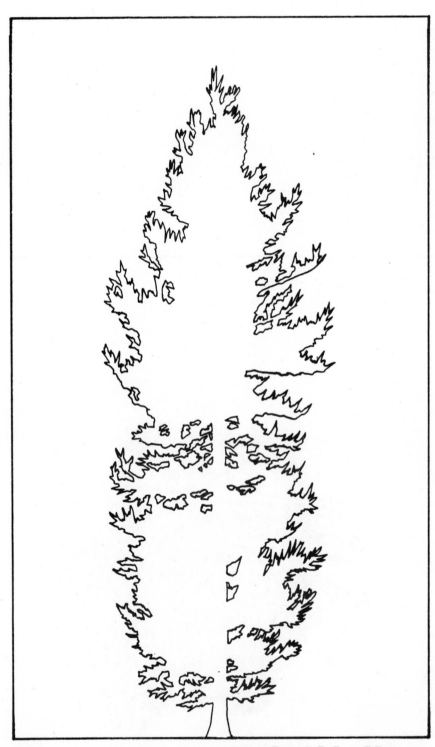

Pinus contorta latifolia

Pinus contorta latifolia

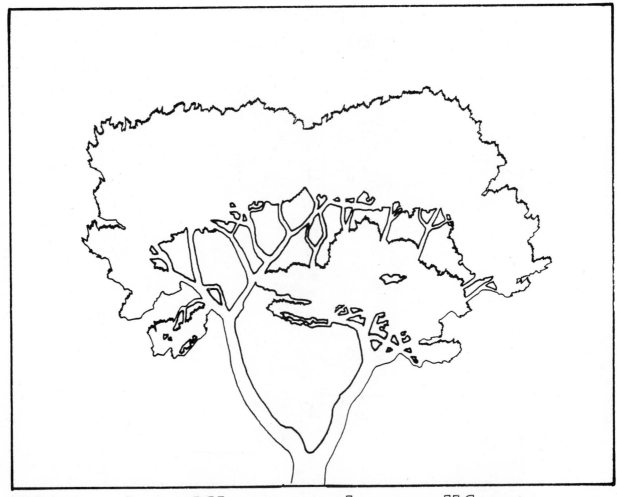

Pinus densiflora umbraculifera

Pinus densiflora umbraculifera

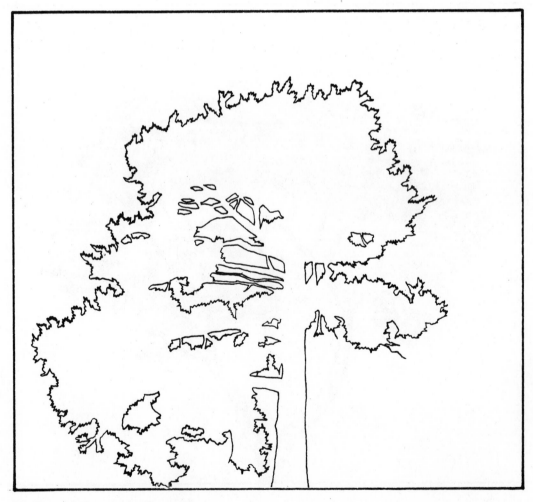

Pinus edulis

Pinus edulis

Pinus halepensis

Pinus halepensis

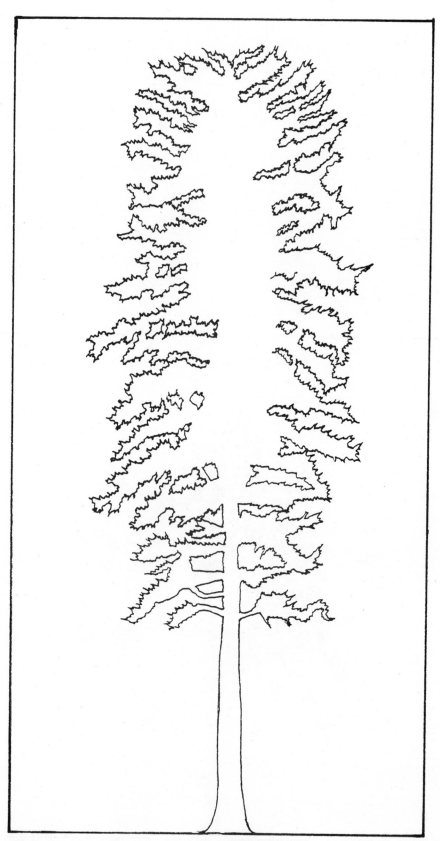

Pinus lambertiana

Pinus lambertiana

Pinus montezumae

Pinus montezumae

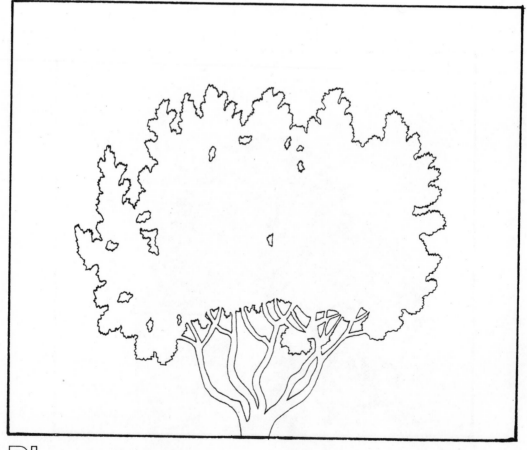

Pinus mugo

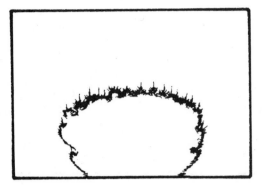 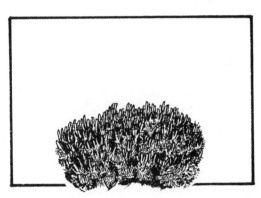

Pinus mugo mughus

Pinus mugo

Pinus muricata

Pinus muricata

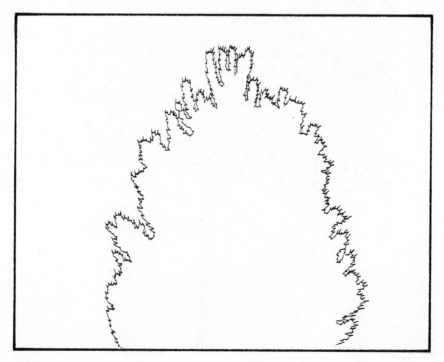

Pinus nigra (immature)

Pinus nigra (immature)

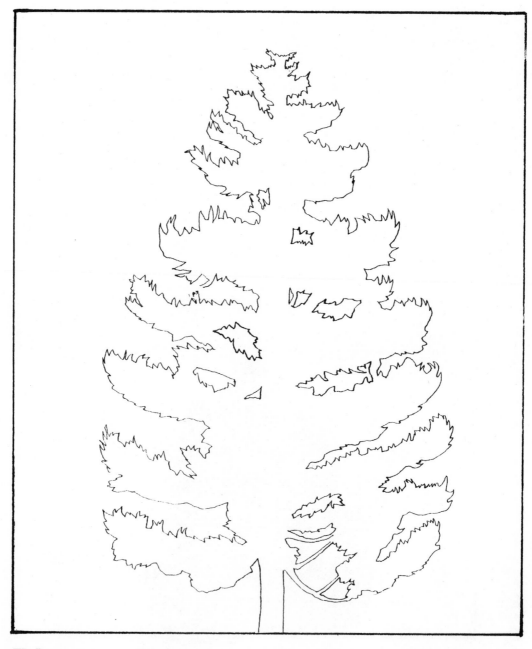

Pinus nigra (mature)

Pinus nigra (mature)

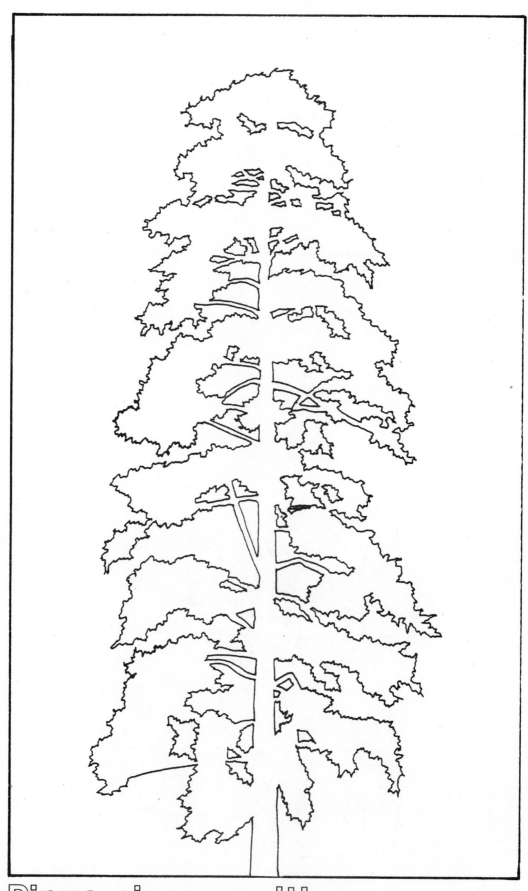

Pinus nigra maritima

Pinus nigra maritima

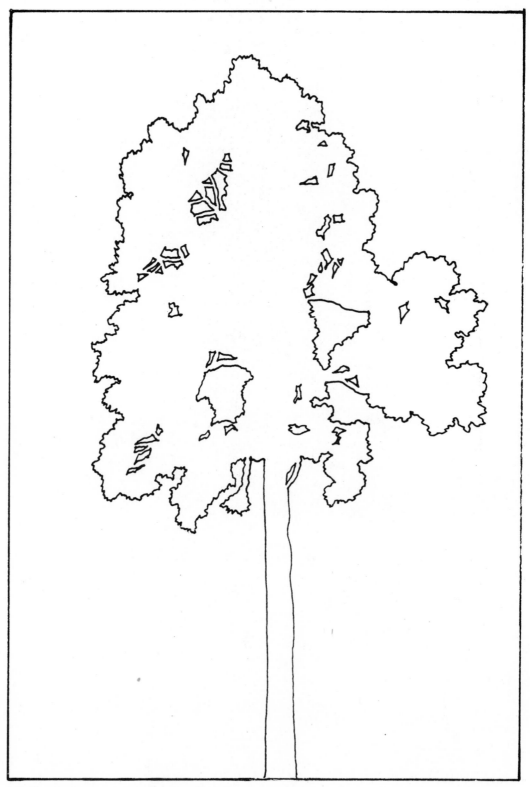

Pinus palustris

Pinus palustris

Pinus parviflora

Pinus parviflora

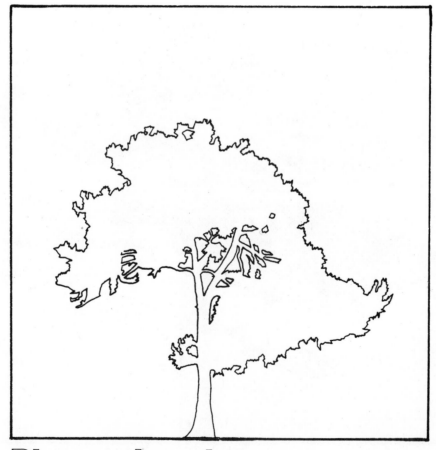

Pinus pinaster

Pinus pinaster

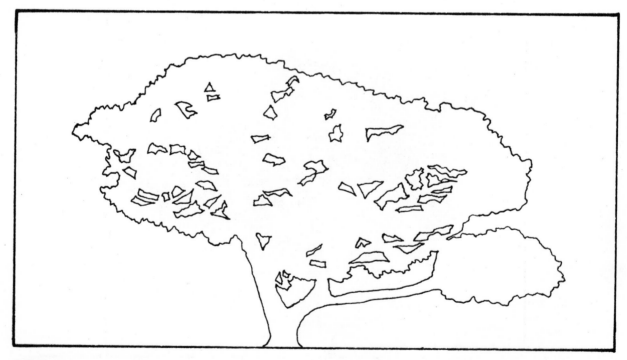

Pinus pinea

Pinus pinea

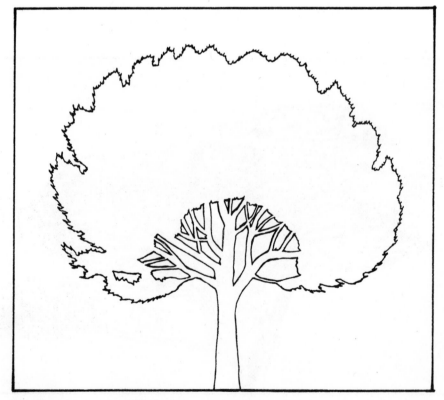

Pinus pinea

Pinus pinea

173

Pinus pinea

Pinus pinea

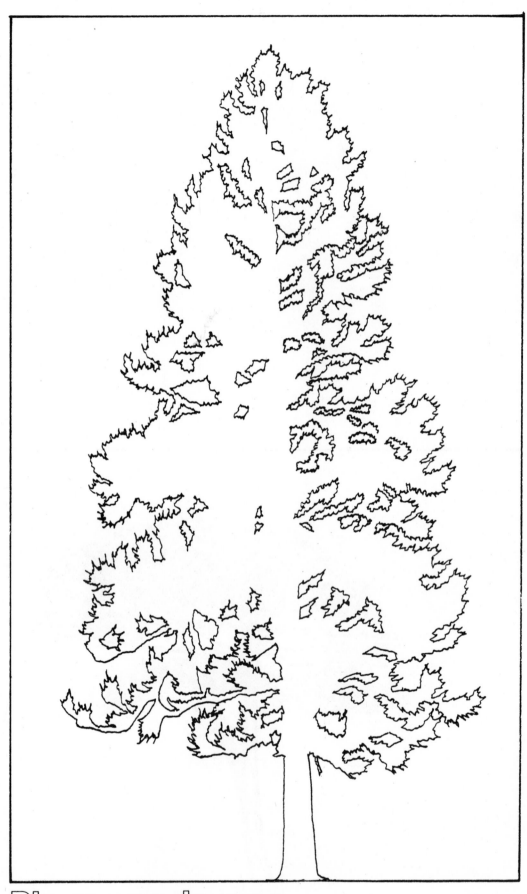

Pinus ponderosa

Pinus ponderosa

Pinus radiata

Pinus radiata

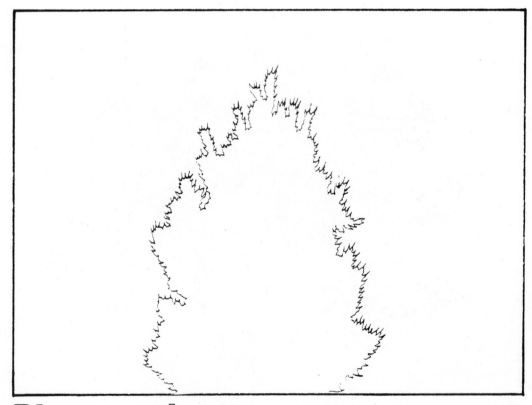

Pinus resinosa (immature)

Pinus resinosa (immature)

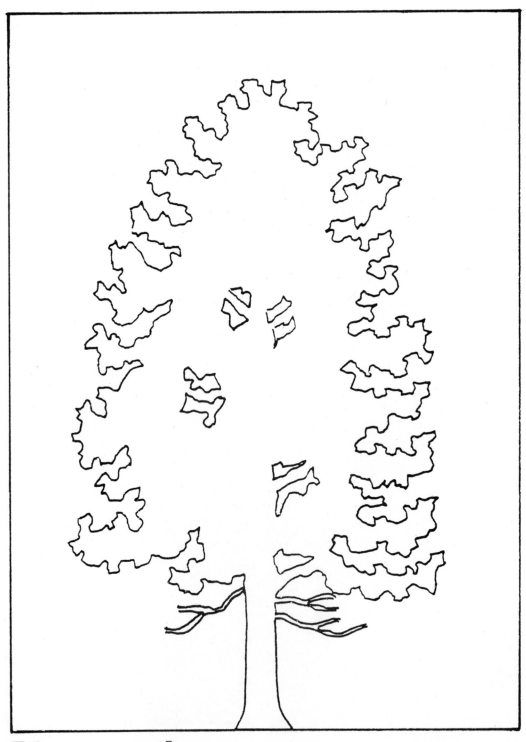

Pinus resinosa (mature)

Pinus resinosa (mature)

Pinus rigida

Pinus rigida

Pinus rigida

Pinus rigida

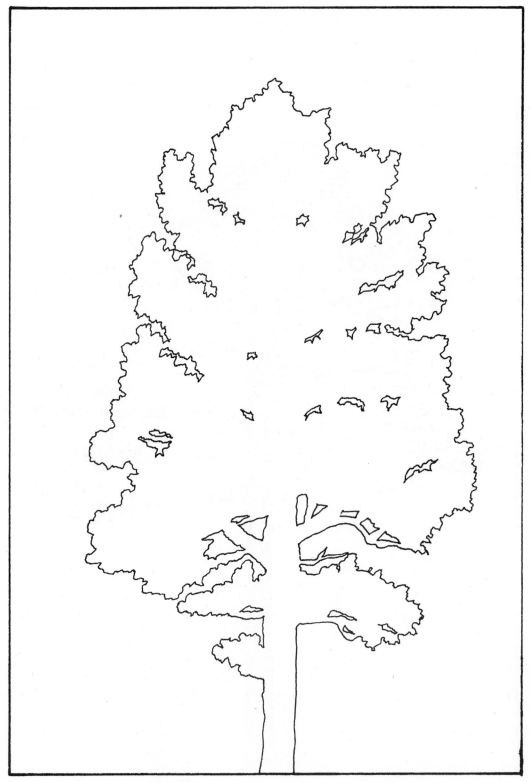

Pinus rigida

Pinus rigida

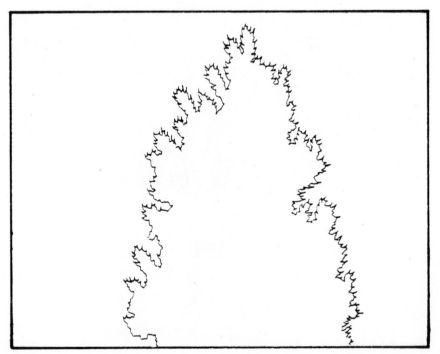

Pinus strobus (immature)

Pinus strobus (immature)

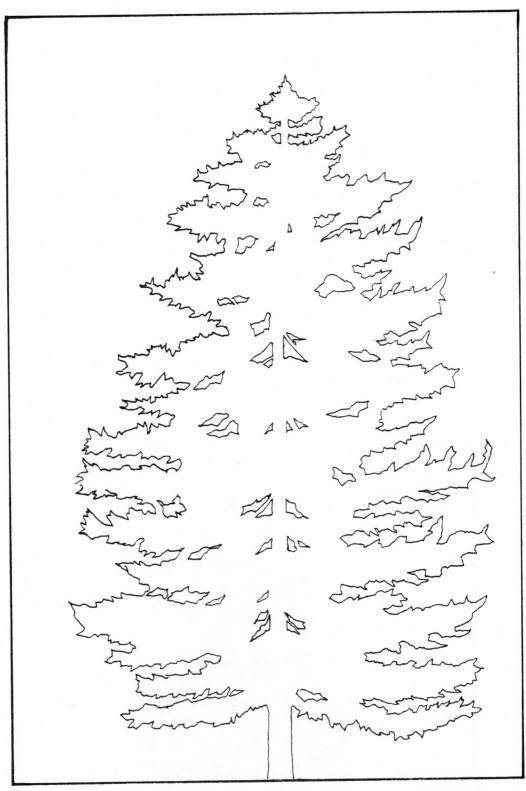

Pinus strobus

Pinus strobus

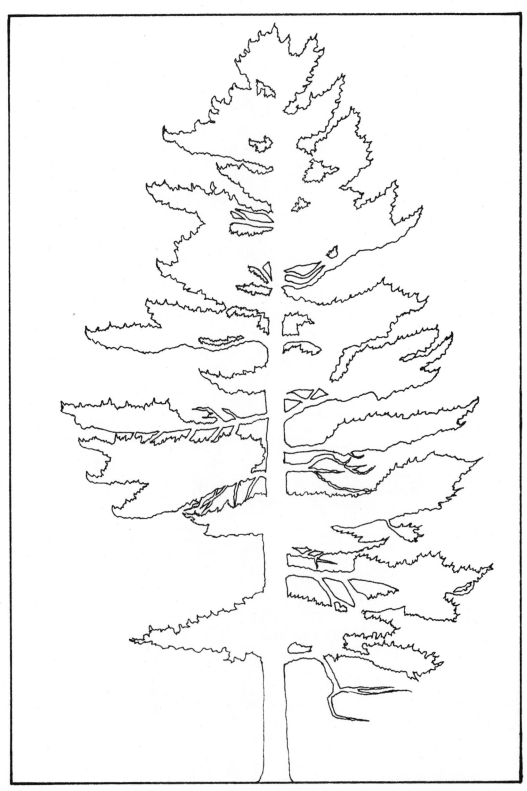

Pinus strobus (mature)

Pinus strobus (mature)

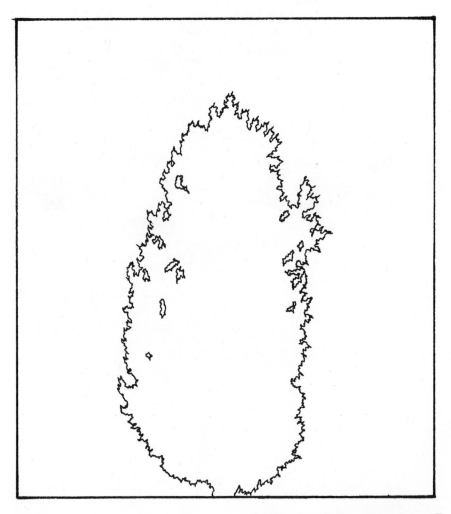

Pinus strobus `Fastigiata´

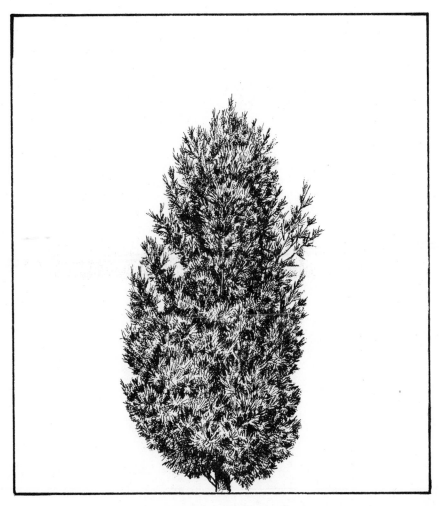

Pinus strobus `Fastigiata´

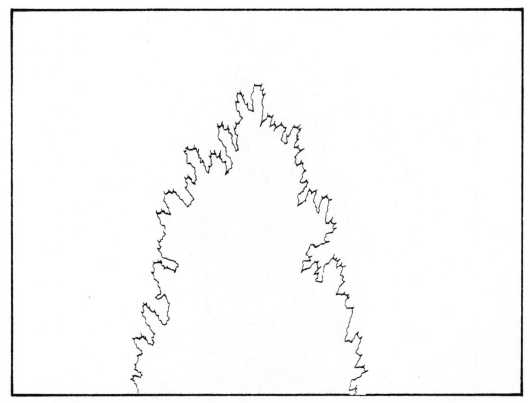

Pinus sylvestris (immature)

Pinus sylvestris (immature)

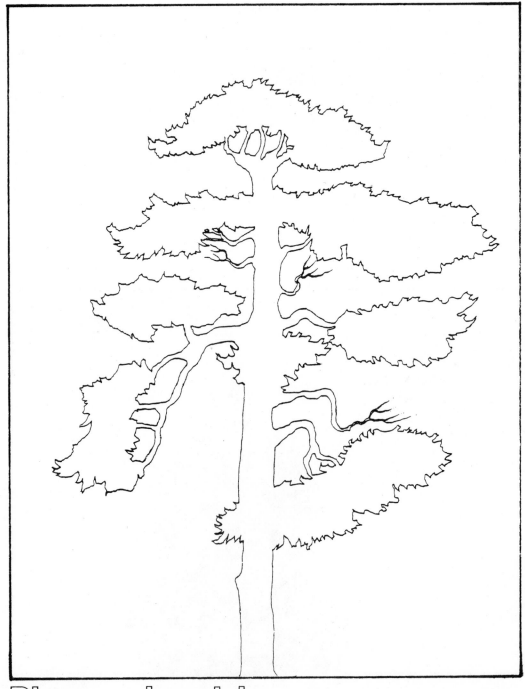

Pinus sylvestris (mature)

Pinus sylvestris (mature)

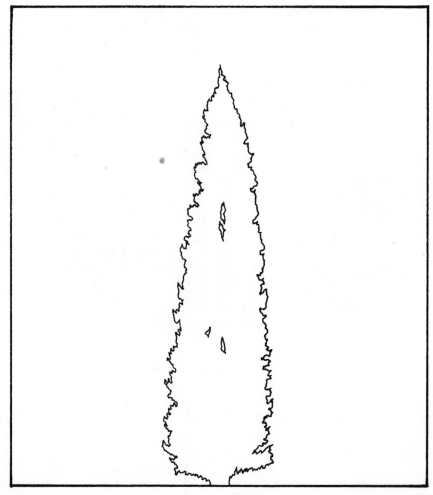

Pinus sylvestris `Fastigiata´

Pinus sylvestris `Fastigiata´

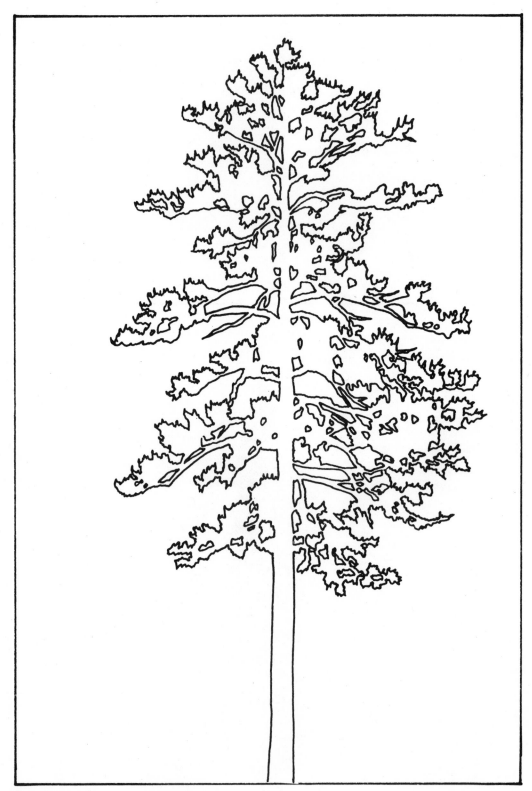

Pinus taeda

Pinus taeda

Pinus thunbergi

Pinus thunbergi

Pinus thunbergi

Pinus thunbergi

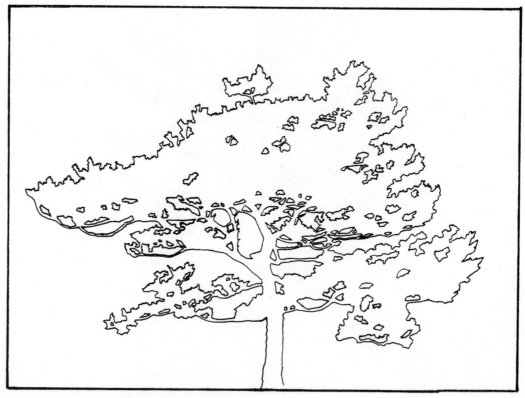

Pinus thunbergi

Pinus thunbergi

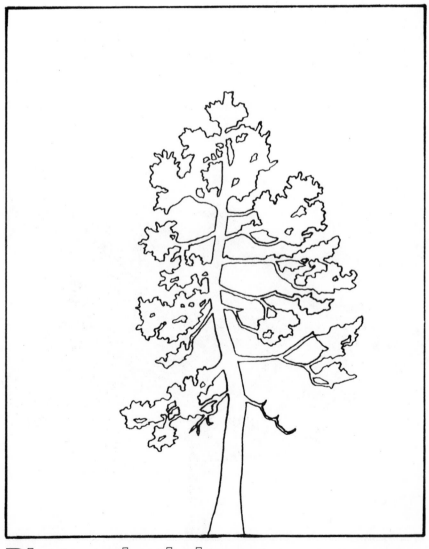

Pinus virginiana

Pinus virginiana

Podocarpus gracilior

Podocarpus gracilior

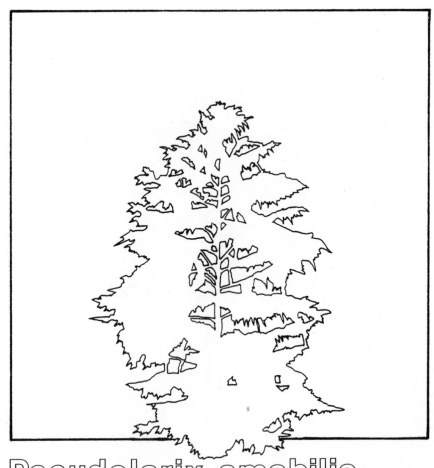

Pseudolarix amabilis

Pseudolarix amabilis

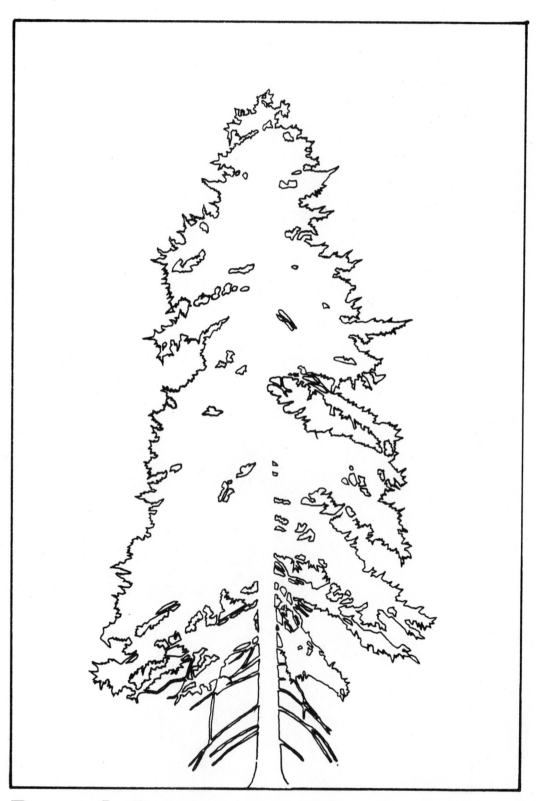

Pseudotsuga menziesii

Pseudotsuga menziesii

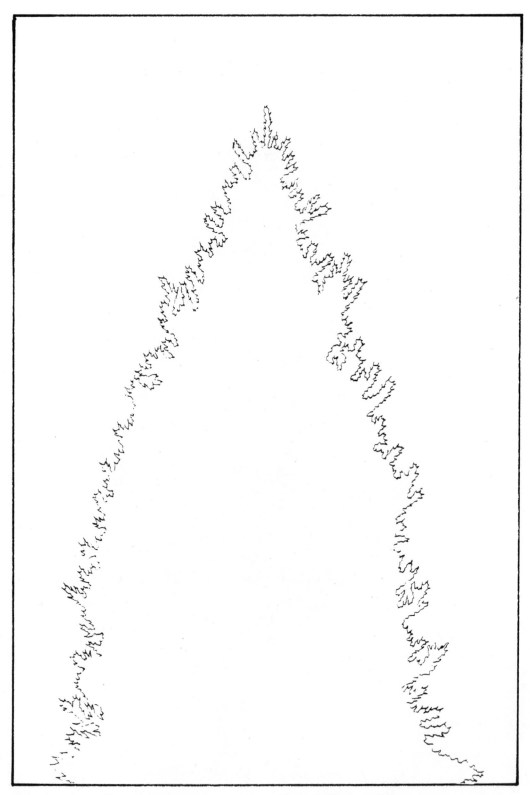

Pseudotsuga menziesii

Pseudotsuga menziesii

221

Sciadopitys verticillata

222

Sciadopitys verticillata

223

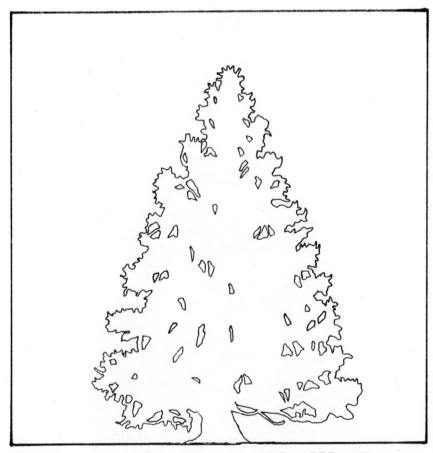

Sciadopitys verticillata

Sciadopitys verticillata

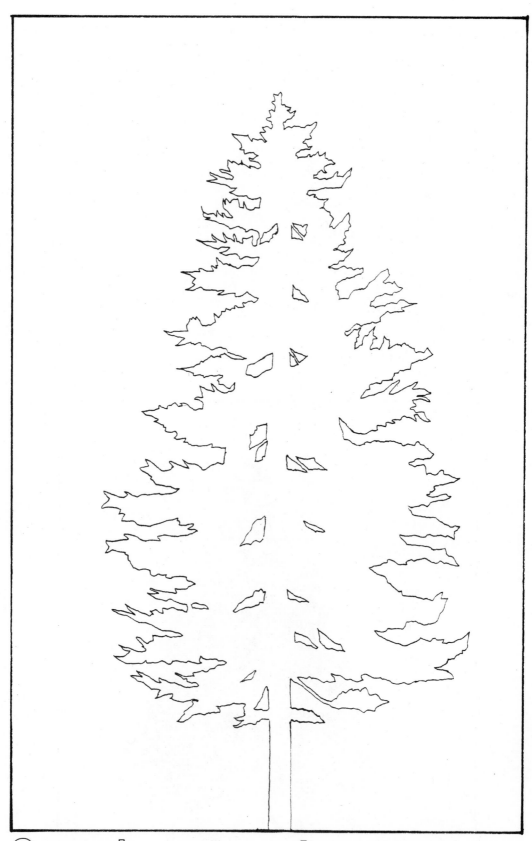

Sequoia sempervirens

Sequoia sempervirens

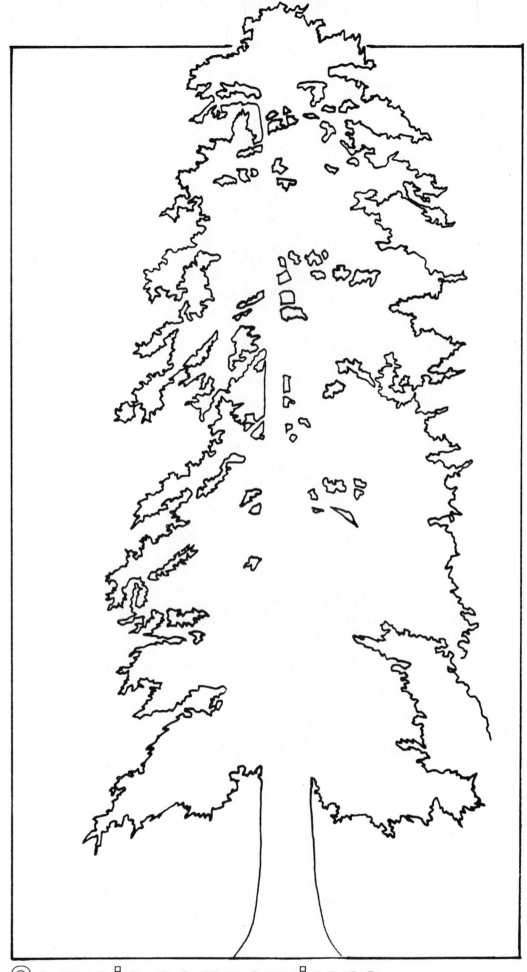

Sequoia sempervirens

Sequoia sempervirens

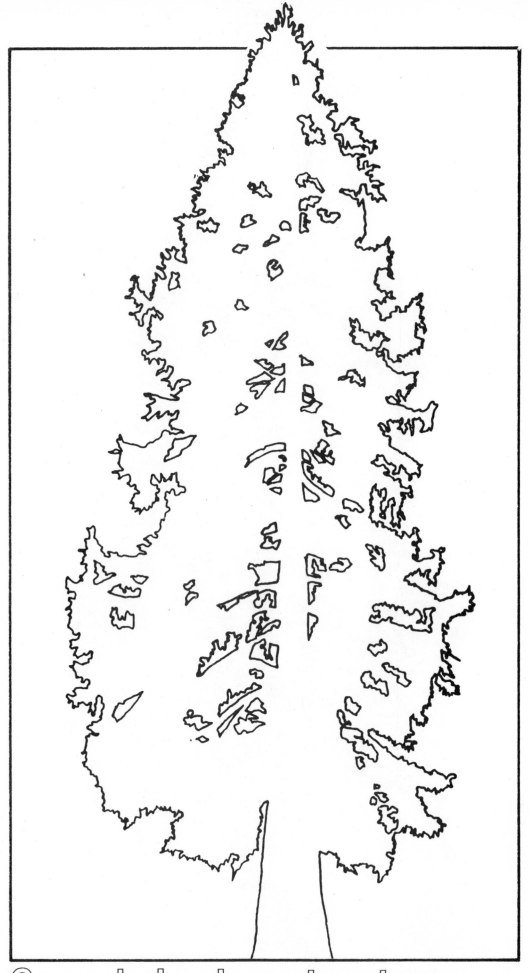

Sequoiadendron giganteum

Sequoiadendron giganteum

231

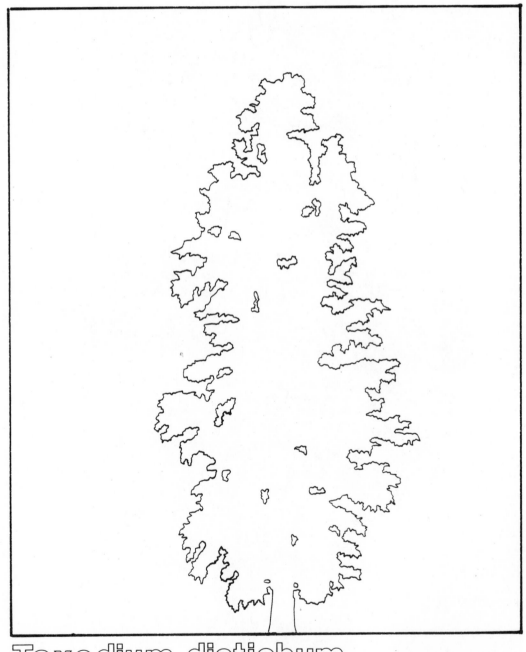

Taxodium distichum

Taxodium distichum

Taxodium distichum

234

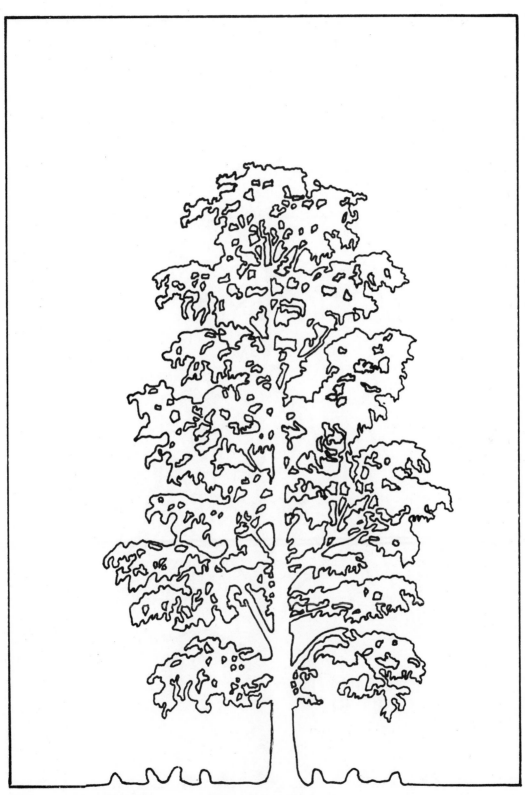

Taxodium distichum

Taxodium distichum

Taxodium distichum

Taxodium distichum

Taxodium distichum

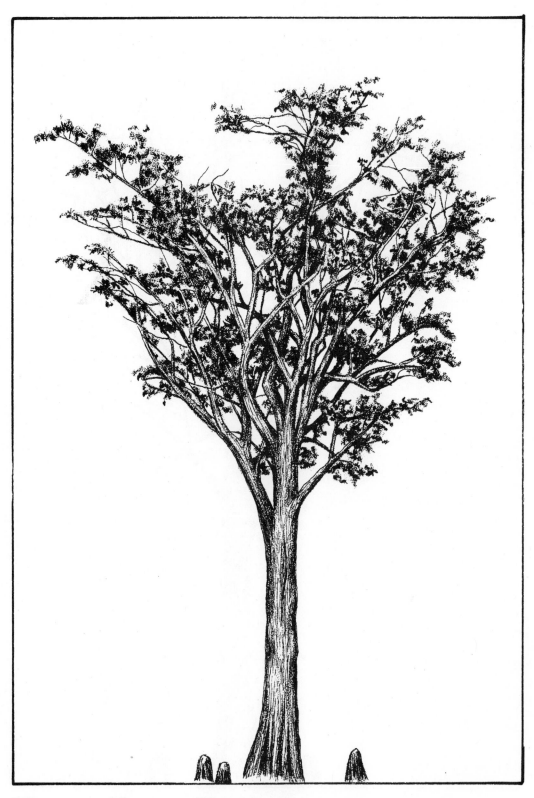

Taxodium distichum

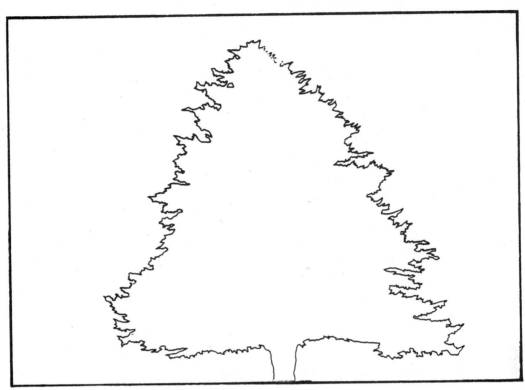

Taxus baccata

Taxus baccata

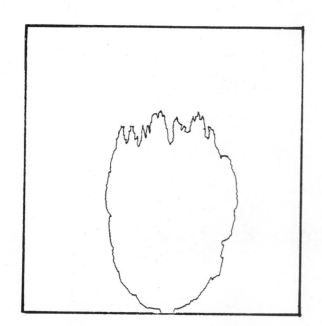 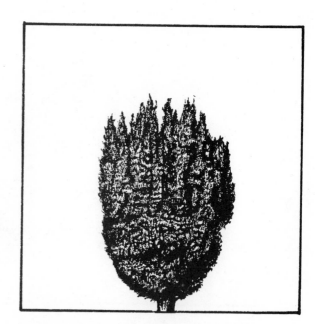

Taxus baccata `Fastigiata´

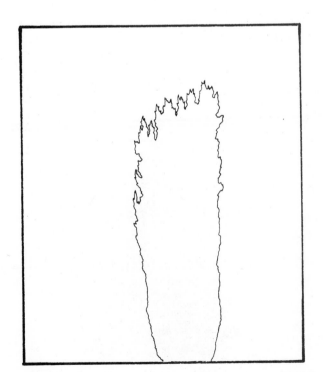 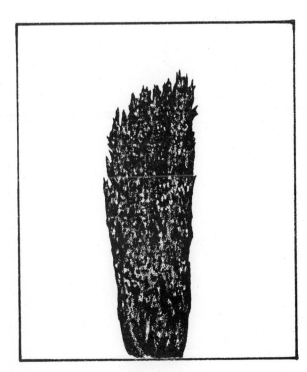

Taxus baccata `Fastigiata´

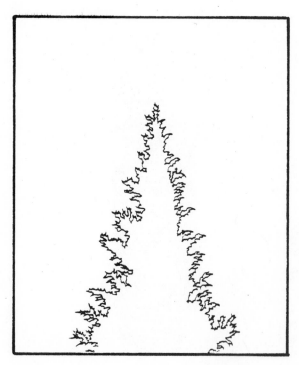 

Taxus cuspidata `Capitata´

Taxus canadensis

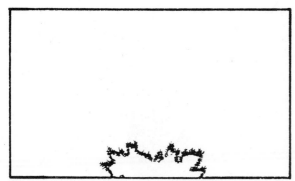
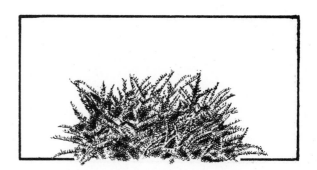

Taxus cuspidata

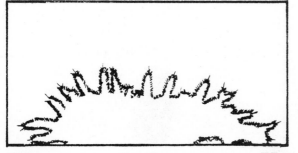

Taxus cuspidata `Nana´

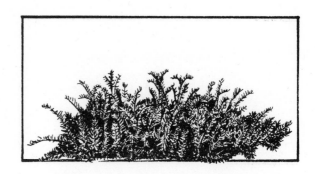

Taxus intermedia

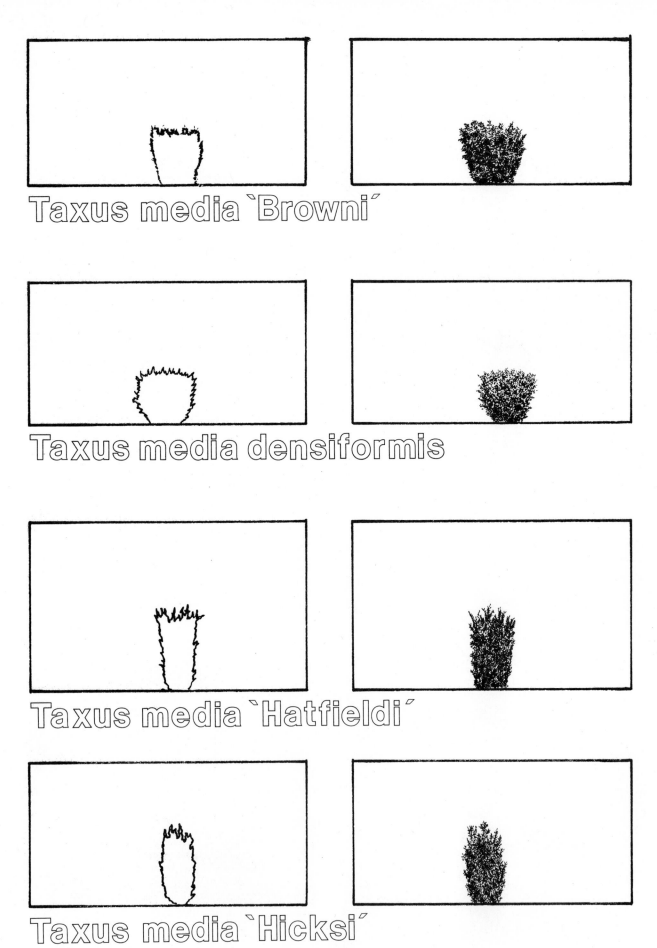

Taxus media `Browni´

Taxus media densiformis

Taxus media `Hatfieldi´

Taxus media `Hicksi´

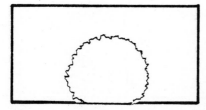 

Thuja occidentalis `Globosa´

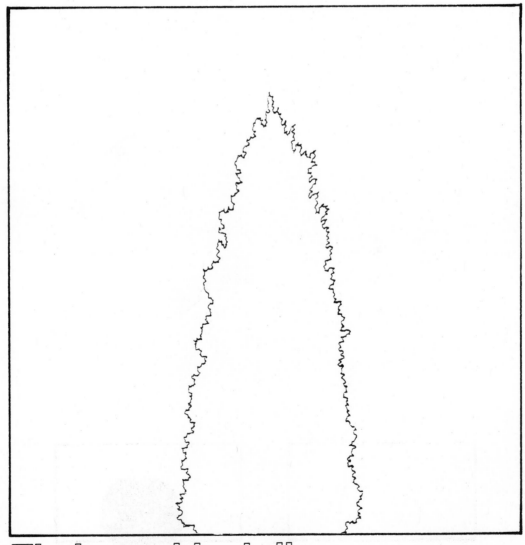

Thuja occidentalis

Thuja occidentalis

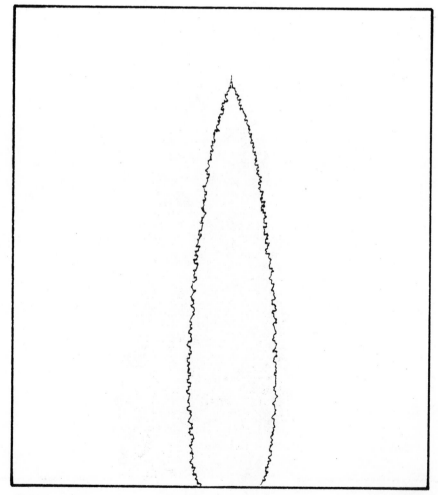

Thuja occidentalis `Fastigiata´

Thuja occidentalis `Fastigiata´

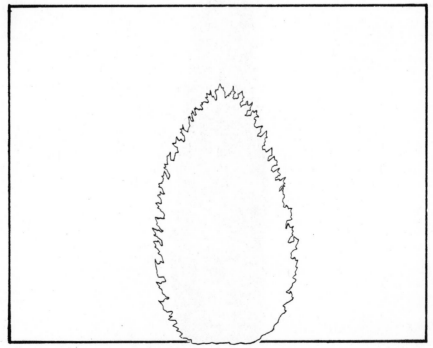

Thuja orientalis

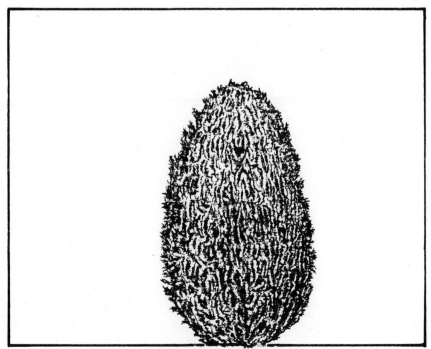

Thuja orientalis

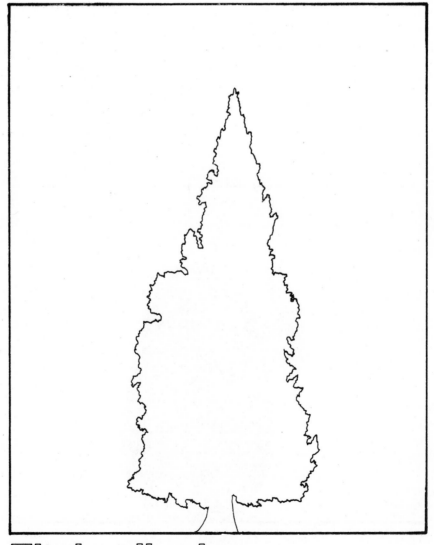

Thuja plicata

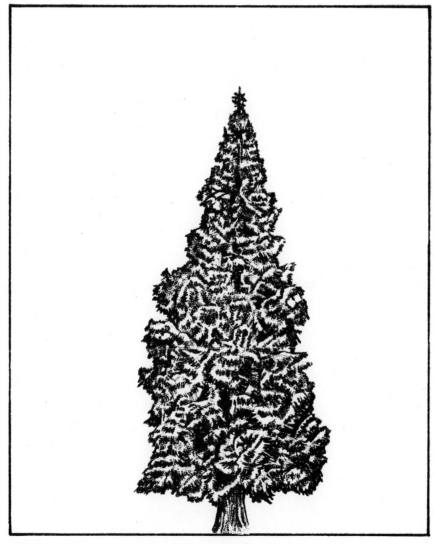

Thuja plicata

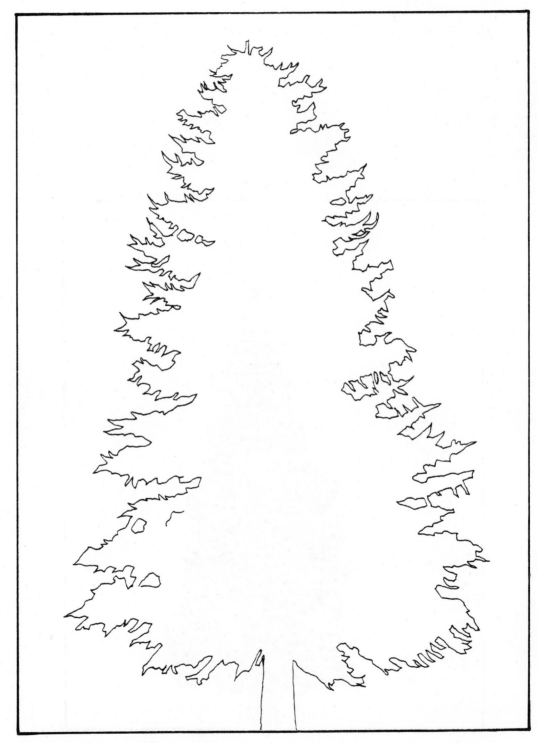

Thuja plicata

Thuja plicata

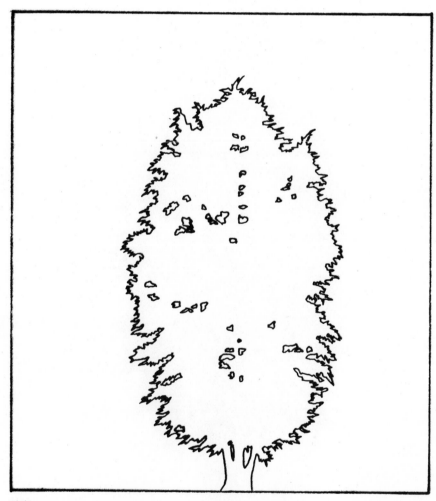

Tsuga canadensis

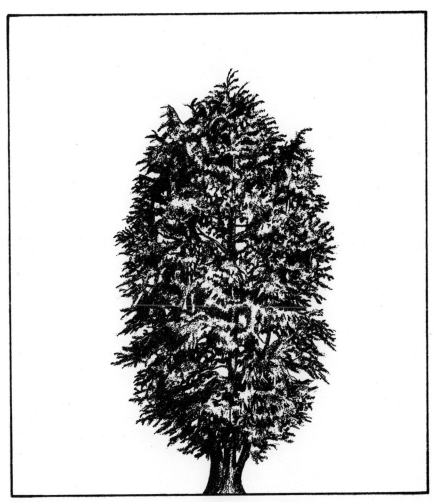

Tsuga canadensis

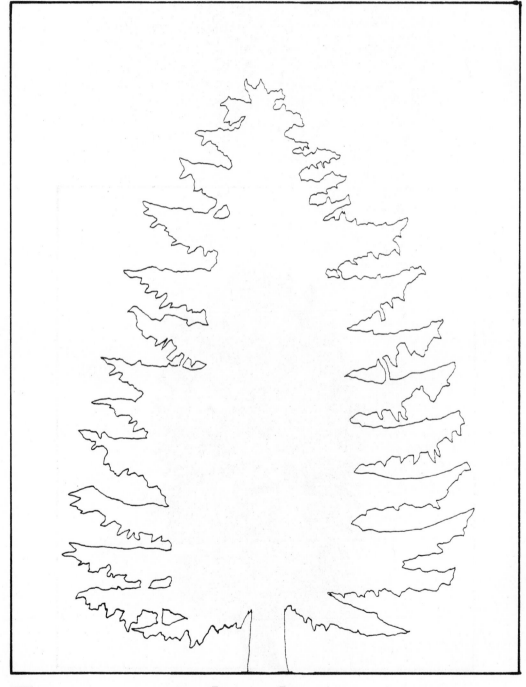

Tsuga canadensis

Tsuga canadensis

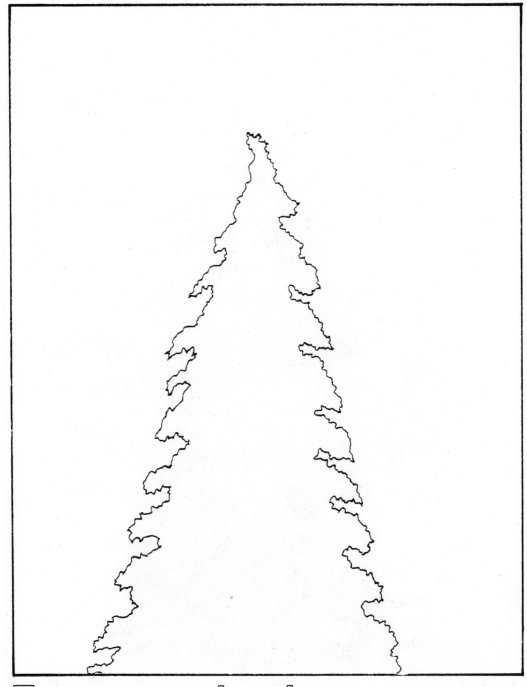

Tsuga canadensis

Tsuga canadensis

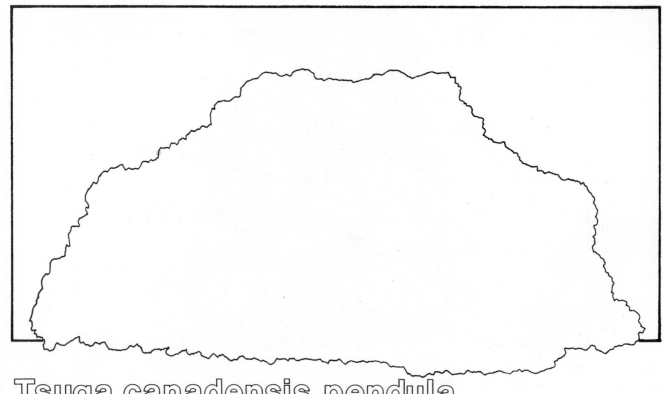

Tsuga canadensis pendula

canadensis pendula

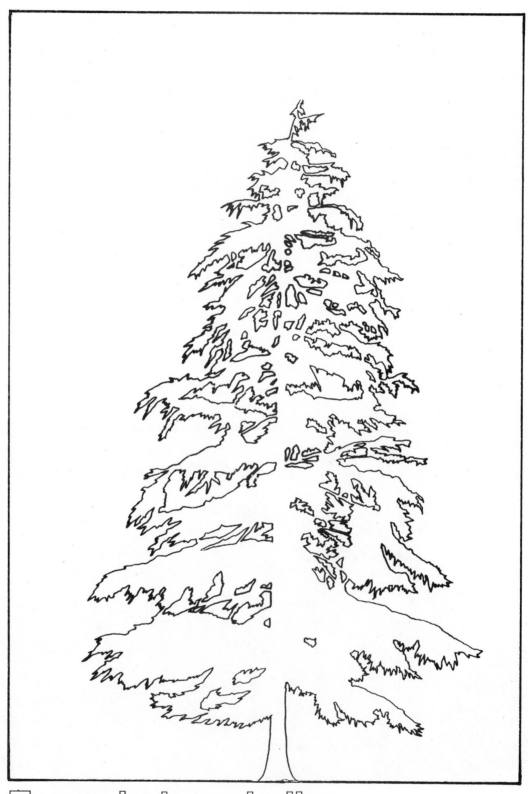

Tsuga heterophylla

Tsuga heterophylla

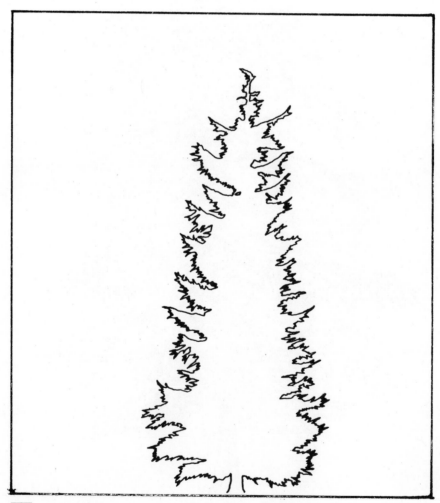

Tsuga mertensiana

Tsuga mertensiana

CYPRESSES and CEDARS

*Calocedrus
decurrens*

*Cedrus
attantica*

*Cedrus
deodora*

*Cedrus
libani*

*Chamaecyparis
lawsoniana*

*Chamaecyparis
lawsoniana*

Chamaecyparis nootkatensis

Chamaecyparis pisifera

Cryptomeria japonica

Cryptomeria japonica

Cryptomeria japonica elegans

Cupressocyparis leylandi

Cupressus glabra

Cupressus macrocarpa

Cupressus macrocarpa

Cupressus
macrocarpa

Cupressus
macrocarpa

Cupressus
sempervirens
'Columnar'

Cupressus
sempervirens
'Columnare'

Thuja
occidentalis

Thuja
occidentalis

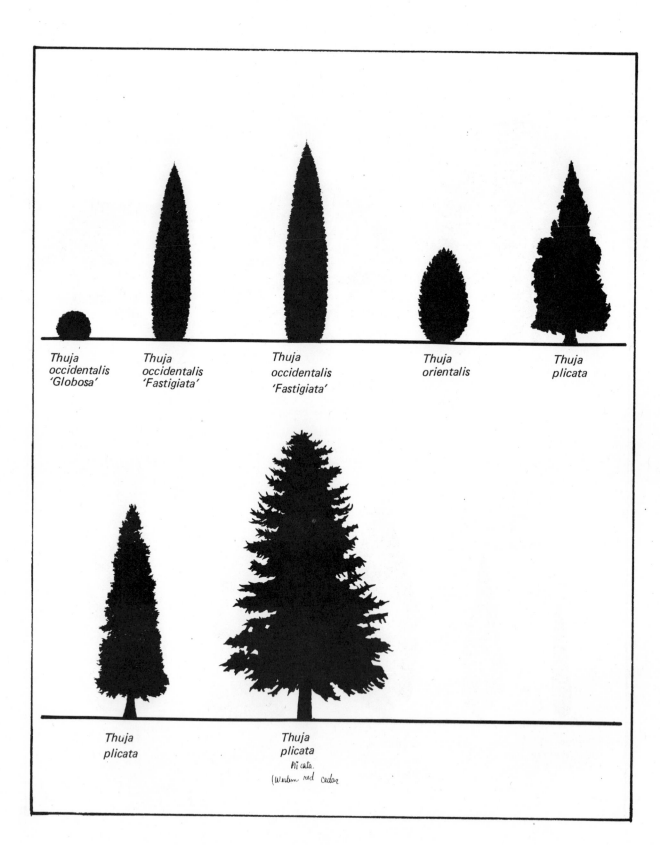

Thuja
occidentalis
'Globosa'

Thuja
occidentalis
'Fastigiata'

Thuja
occidentalis
'Fastigiata'

Thuja
orientalis

Thuja
plicata

Thuja
plicata

Thuja
plicata

Plicata.
(Western red cedar

276

Abies
alba

Abies
amabilis

Abies
balsamae

Abies
balsamae

Abies
concolor

Abies
grandis

Abies
koreana

Abies
nordmanniana

Abies
procera

Cunninghamia
lanceolota

Picea
abies

Picea
abies

Picea
brewerana

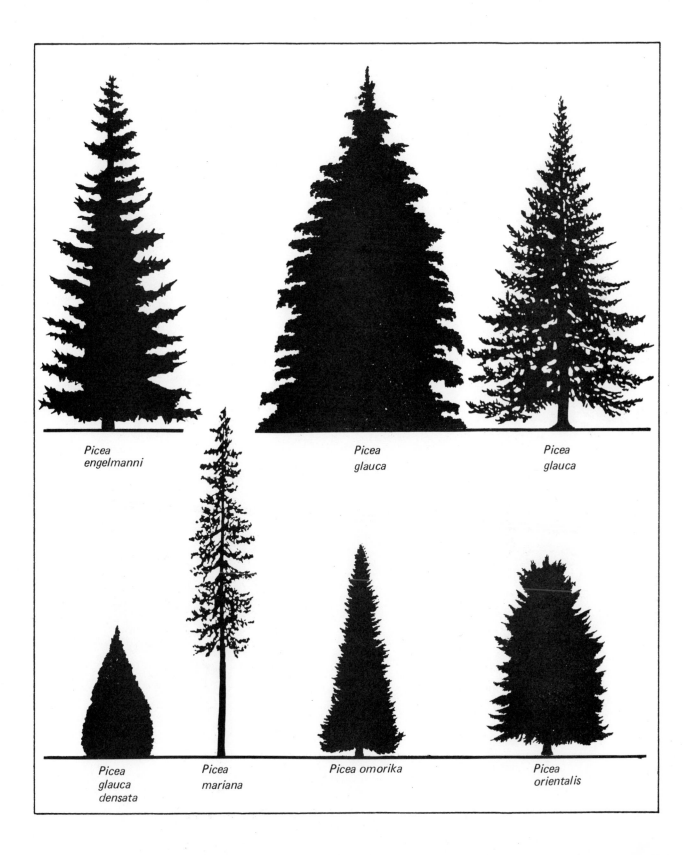

Picea
engelmanni

Picea
glauca

Picea
glauca

Picea
glauca
densata

Picea
mariana

Picea omorika

Picea
orientalis

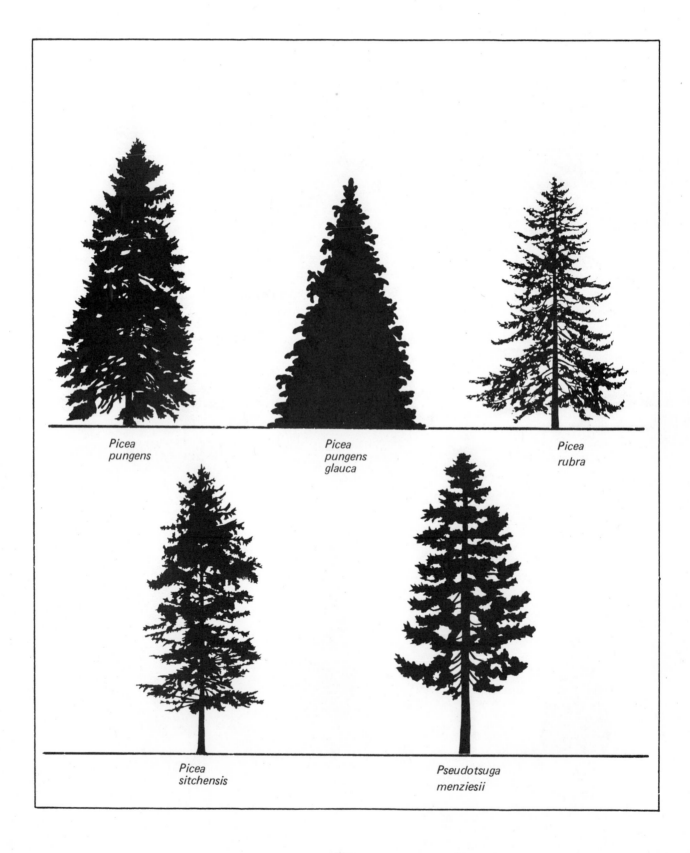

Picea
pungens

Picea
pungens
glauca

Picea
rubra

Picea
sitchensis

Pseudotsuga
menziesii

*Pseudotsuga
menziesii*

*Pseudotsuga
menziesii*

*Pseudotsuga
menziesii*

281

HEMLOCKS

Tsuga
canadensis

Taxus
canadensis

Taxus
canadensis

Tsuga
canadensis

Tsuga canadensis pendula

Tsuga
caroliniana

Tsuga
heterophylla

Tsuga
mertensiana

JUNIPERS

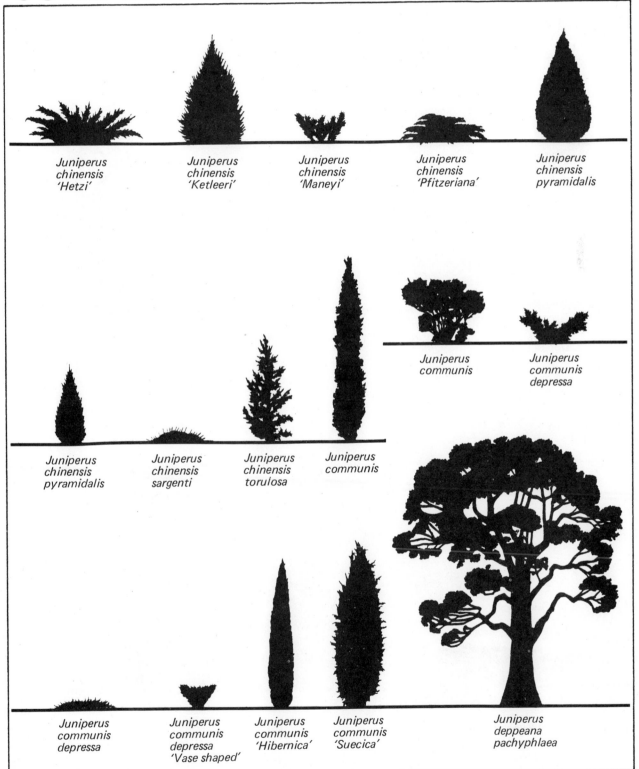

Juniperus
chinensis
'Hetzi'

Juniperus
chinensis
'Ketleeri'

Juniperus
chinensis
'Maneyi'

Juniperus
chinensis
'Pfitzeriana'

Juniperus
chinensis
pyramidalis

Juniperus
communis

Juniperus
communis
depressa

Juniperus
chinensis
pyramidalis

Juniperus
chinensis
sargenti

Juniperus
chinensis
torulosa

Juniperus
communis

Juniperus
communis
depressa

Juniperus
communis
depressa
'Vase shaped'

Juniperus
communis
'Hibernica'

Juniperus
communis
'Suecica'

Juniperus
deppeana
pachyphlaea

*Juniperus
excelsa
stricta*

*Juniperus
horizontalis*

*Juniperus
horizontalis
'Bar Harbor'*

*Juniperus
horizontalis
'Douglasi'*

*Juniperus
horizontalis
'Plumosa'*

*Juniperus
horizontalis
'Wiltoni'*

*Juniperus
monosperma*

*Juniperus
procumbens*

*Juniperus
sabina*

*Juniperus
sabina
tamariscifolia*

*Juniperus
sabina
'Vonehron'*

*Juniperus
scopulorum*

*Juniperus
squamata
'Meyeri'*

*Juniperus
virginiana*

*Juniperus
virginiana*

*Juniperus
virginiana*

*Juniperus
virginiana*

*Juniperus
virginiana
'Canaerti'*

*Juniperus
virginiana
'Glauca'*

*Juniperus
virginiana
'Hilli'*

LARCH,DAWN REDWOOD and BALD CYPRESS

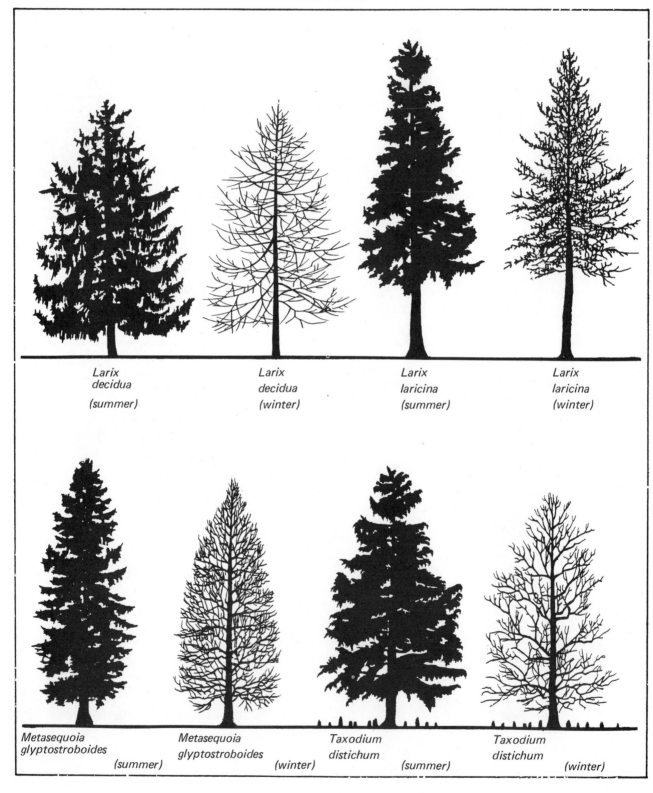

*Larix
decidua*

(summer)

*Larix
decidua*

(winter)

*Larix
laricina*

(summer)

*Larix
laricina*

(winter)

*Metasequoia
glyptostroboides*

(summer)

*Metasequoia
glyptostroboides*

(winter)

*Taxodium
distichum*

(summer)

*Taxodium
distichum*

(winter)

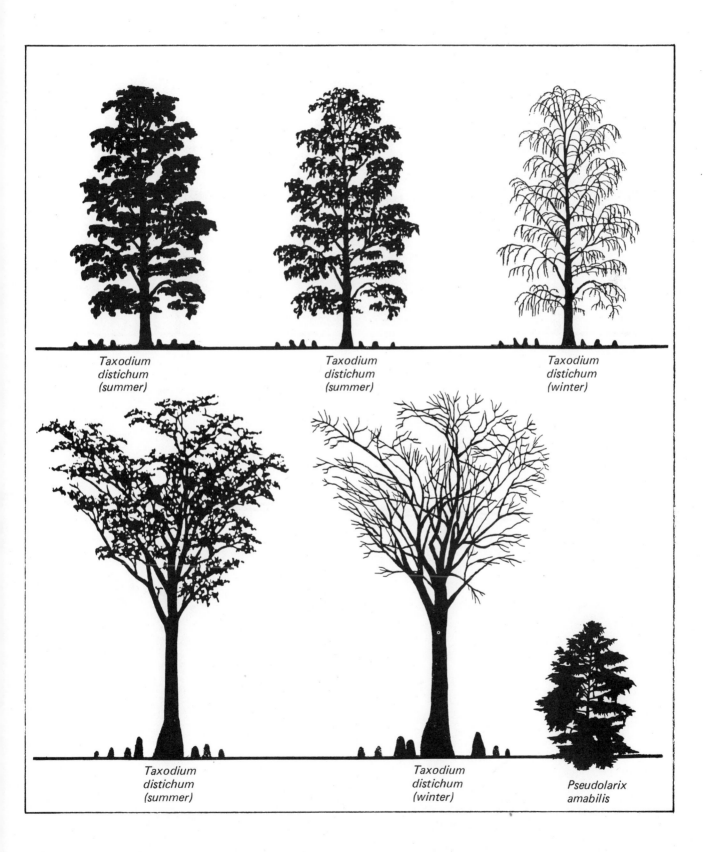

*Taxodium
distichum
(summer)*

*Taxodium
distichum
(summer)*

*Taxodium
distichum
(winter)*

*Taxodium
distichum
(summer)*

*Taxodium
distichum
(winter)*

*Pseudolarix
amabilis*

MONKEY PUZZLE TREE
and SWAMP SHE OAK

*Araucaria
araucana*

*Araucaria
araucana*

*Casuarina
equisitifolia*

PINES

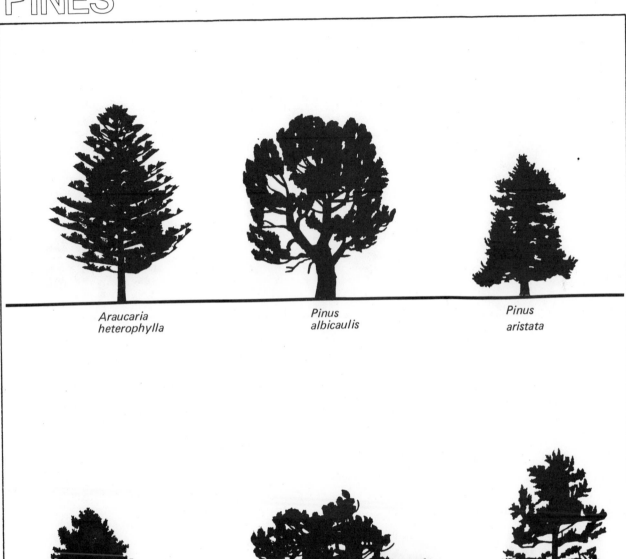

Araucaria
heterophylla

Pinus
albicaulis

Pinus
aristata

Pinus
ayacahuite

Pinus
balfouriana

Pinus
banksiana

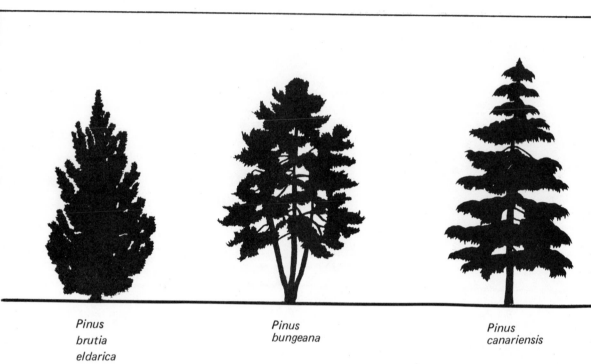

Pinus
brutia
eldarica

Pinus
bungeana

Pinus
canariensis

Pinus
cembra

Pinus
cembra

Pinus
cembroides

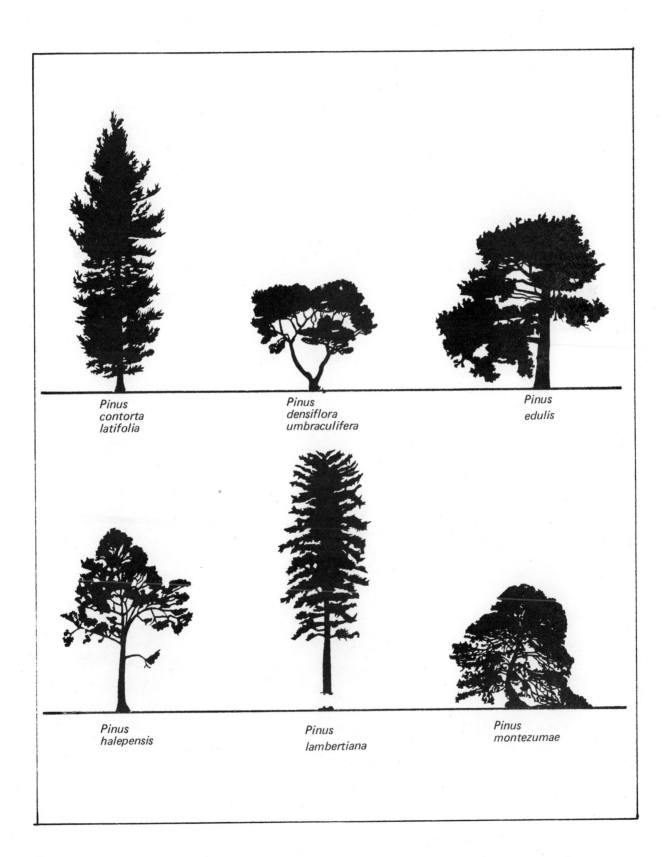

Pinus
contorta
latifolia

Pinus
densiflora
umbraculifera

Pinus
edulis

Pinus
halepensis

Pinus
lambertiana

Pinus
montezumae

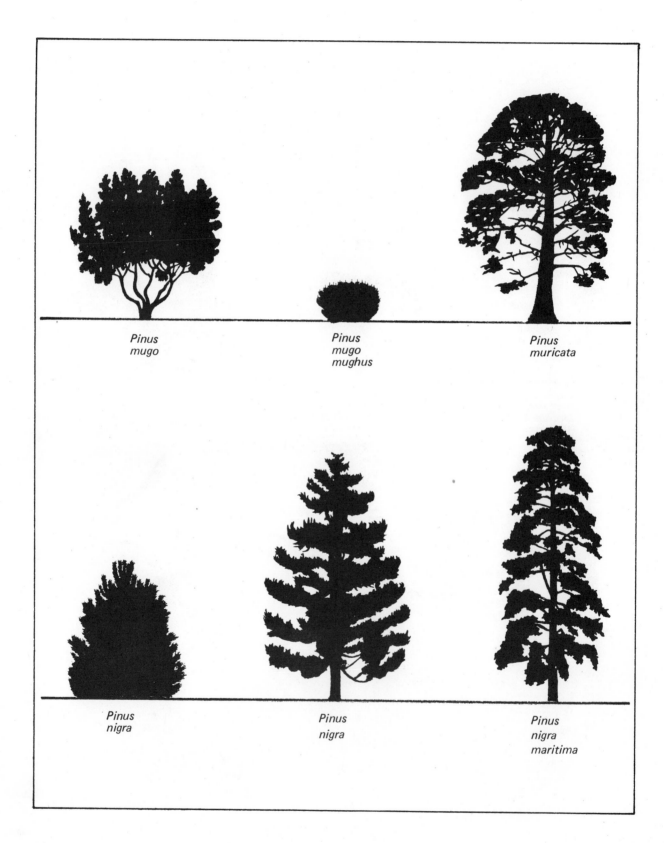

Pinus
mugo

Pinus
mugo
mughus

Pinus
muricata

Pinus
nigra

Pinus
nigra

Pinus
nigra
maritima

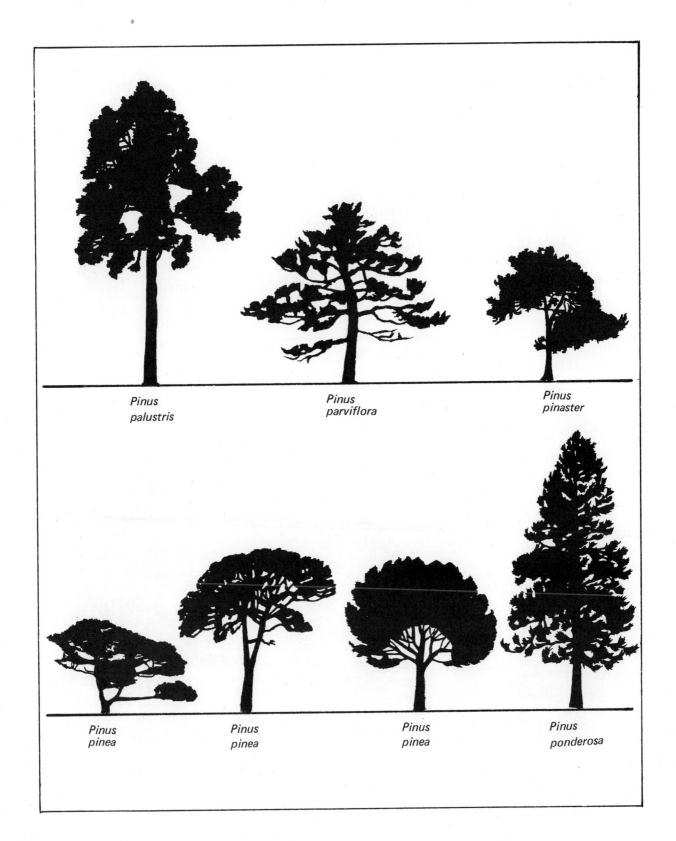

Pinus
palustris

Pinus
parviflora

Pinus
pinaster

Pinus
pinea

Pinus
pinea

Pinus
pinea

Pinus
ponderosa

Pinus
radiata

Pinus
radiata

Pinus
radiata

Pinus
resinosa

Pinus
resinosa

Pinus
resinosa

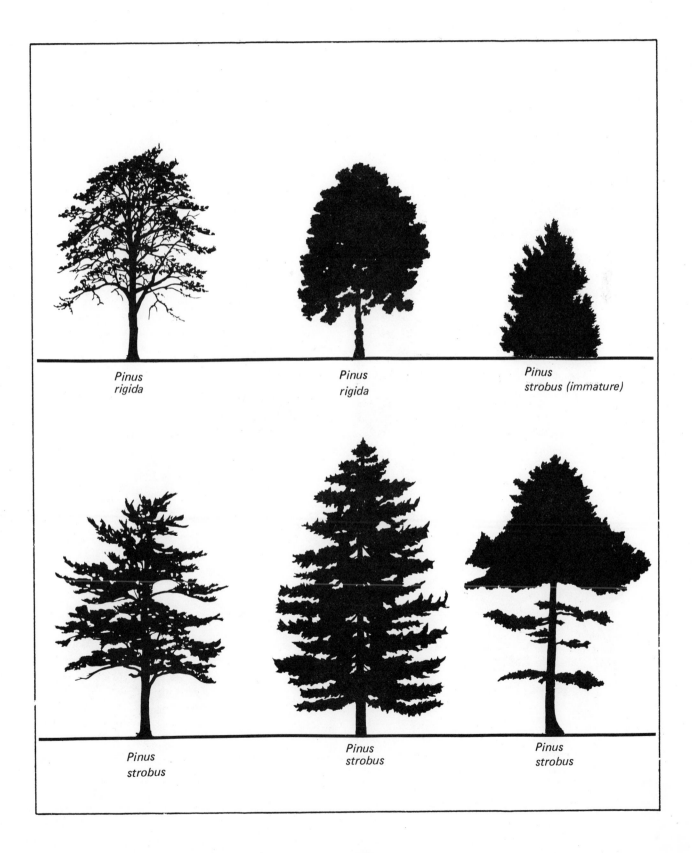

Pinus
rigida

Pinus
rigida

Pinus
strobus (immature)

Pinus
strobus

Pinus
strobus

Pinus
strobus

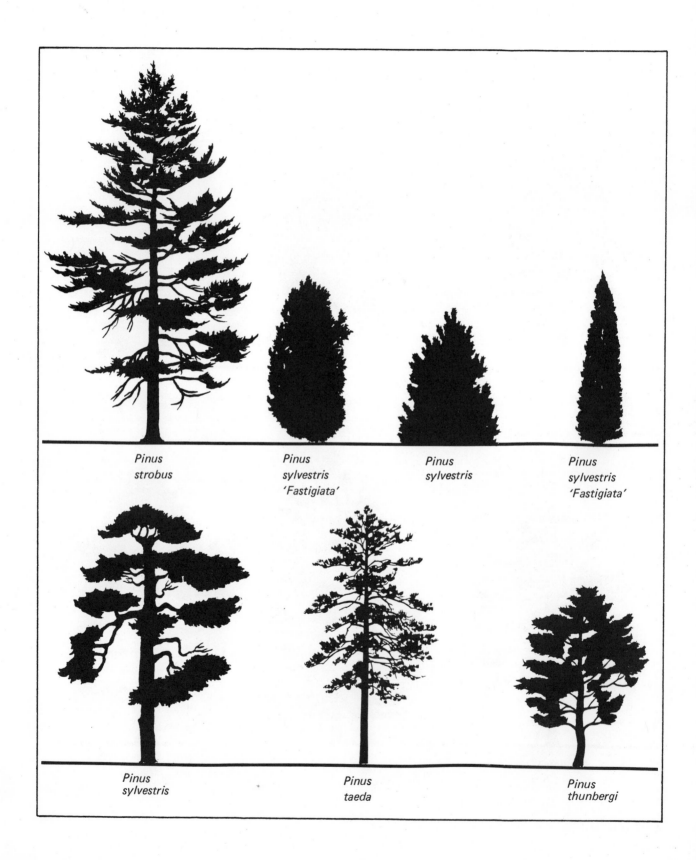

Pinus
strobus

Pinus
sylvestris
'Fastigiata'

Pinus
sylvestris

Pinus
sylvestris
'Fastigiata'

Pinus
sylvestris

Pinus
taeda

Pinus
thunbergi

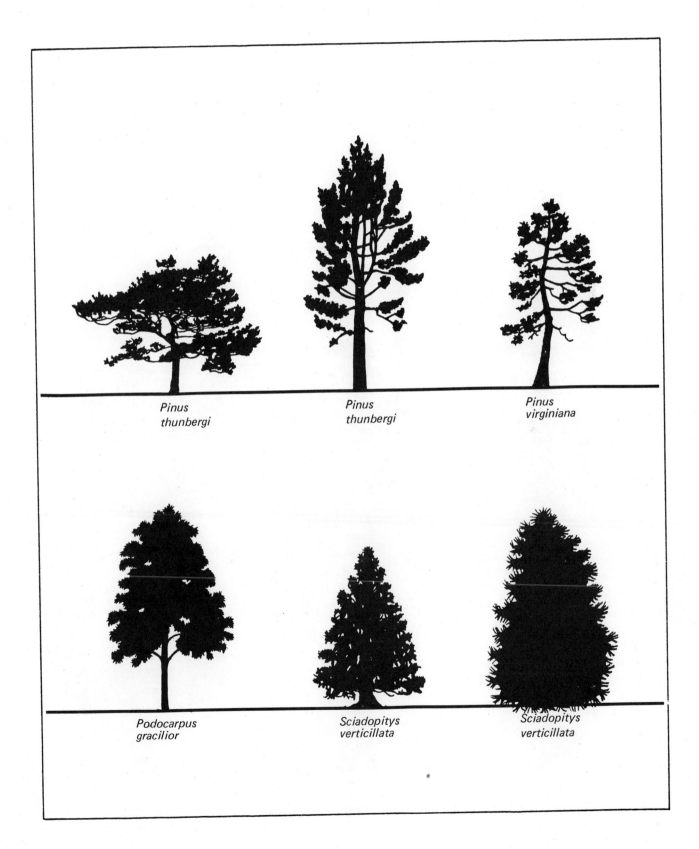

*Pinus
thunbergi*

*Pinus
thunbergi*

*Pinus
virginiana*

*Podocarpus
gracilior*

*Sciadopitys
verticillata*

*Sciadopitys
verticillata*

REDWOOD and SEQUOIA

Sequoia sempervirens (immature)

Sequoia sempervirens   *Sequoiadendron giganteum*   *Sequoiadendron giganteum*

YEWS

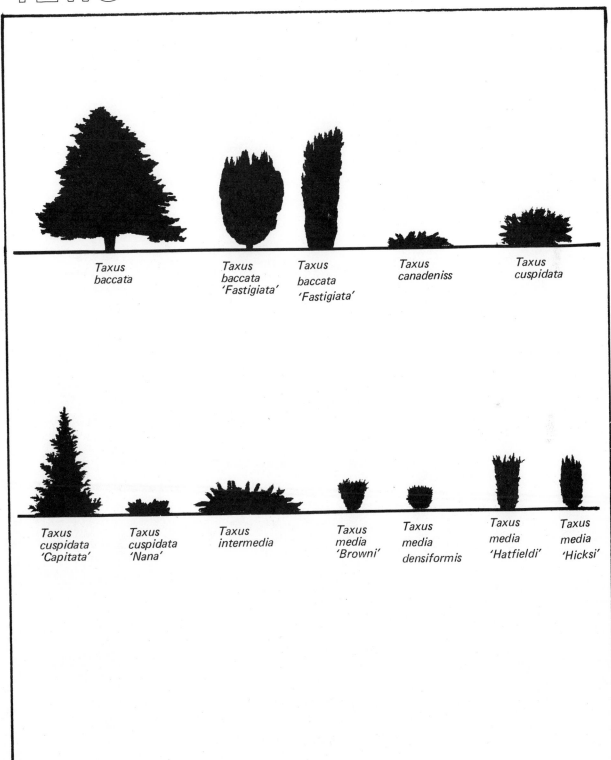

Taxus
baccata

Taxus
baccata
'Fastigiata'

Taxus
baccata
'Fastigiata'

Taxus
canadeniss

Taxus
cuspidata

Taxus
cuspidata
'Capitata'

Taxus
cuspidata
'Nana'

Taxus
intermedia

Taxus
media
'Browni'

Taxus
media
densiformis

Taxus
media
'Hatfieldi'

Taxus
media
'Hicksi'

Bibliography

BIBLIOGRAPHY
Evergreen Plant Form Studies

Association for Planning and Regional Reconstruction. **Trees for Town and Country,** Lund Humphries, 12 Bedford Square, London WC1.

Beatty, Russell A. Trees for Lafayette, Northern California Chapter/ASLA Publications Group, San Francisco, CA. 1977

Beckett, Kenneth A. **The Love of Trees,** Distributed in the U.S.A. by Crescent Books, a division of Crown Publishers,Inc., 1975

Boom, B.K. and H. Kleijn, **The Glory of the Tree,** Doubleday and Co., Garden City, N.Y.,1966

Bringham, Charlotte. **Trees in the City,** (Report No. 236), ASPO Planning Advisory Service, American Society of Planning Officials, Chicago, Illinois, 1968.

Brockman, C. Frank. **Trees of North America,** Golden Press, New York, 1979.

Carpenter, Phillip L., Theodore D. Walker and Frederick O. Lamphear. **Plants in the Landscape,** W.H. Freeman and Co., San Francisco, CA., 1975.

Carter, J. Cedric. **Illinois Trees:Selection, Planting and Care,** Illinois Natural History Survey (Circular 51), Urbana, IL.

Clapham, A.R. **The Oxford Book of Trees,** Oxford University Press, London, 1975.

Collingwood, G.H. and Warren D. Brush. **Knowing Your Trees,** The American Forestry Association, Washington, D.C., 1978.

Crockett, James Underwood. **Trees,** Time-Life Books, New York, 1972.

Daniels, Roland. **Street Trees,** Pennsylvania State University, University Park, PA., 1975.

der Boer, Arie, **Flowering Crabapples,** American Association of Nurserymen, Washington, D.C., 1959.

Dirr, Michael A. **Photographic Manual of Woody Landscape Plants,** Stipes Publishing Co., Champaign, IL., 1969.

Editors of Sunset Books. **Basic Gardening Illustrated,** Lane Publishing Co., Menlo Park, CA., 1976.

Editors of Sunset Books. **Garden Trees,** Lane Publishing Co., Menlo Park, CA. 1975.

Editors of Sunset Books. **Ideas for Japanese Gardens,** Lane Publishing Co., Menlo Park, CA., 1968.

Edlin, Herbert and Maurice Nimmo. **The Illustrated Encyclopedia of Trees,** Harmony Books, New York,N.Y., 1978.

Edlin, Herbert. **The Tree Key,** Charles Scribner's Sons, New York, N.Y., 1978.

Eliot, Willard Ayres. **Forest Trees of the Pacific Coast,** G.P. Putnam and Sons, New York, N.Y., 1938.

Faust, Joan Lee(Editor). **The New York Times Book of Trees and Shrubs,** Alfred A. Knopf, New York, N.Y., 1964.

Flemer, William. **Shade and Ornamental Trees in Color,** Grosset and Dunlap, New York, N.Y., 1965.

Graves, Arthur Harmount. **Illustrated Guide to Trees and Shrubs,** Harper and Row, New York, N.Y., 1956.

Green, Charlotte Hilton. **Trees of the South,** The University of North Carolina, Chapel Hill, N.C., 1939.

Hamblin, Stephen F. **Lists of Plant Types for Landscape Planting,** Harvard University Press, Cambridge, MA., 1923.

Hightshoe, Gary L. **Native Trees for Urban and Rural America,** Iowa State University Research Foundation, Ames, IA.

Holliday, Ivan and Ron Hill. **A Field Guide to Australian Trees,** Rigby Limited, Adelaide, Australia, 1969.

Huxley, Anthony. **Evergreen Garden Trees and Shrubs,** Macmillan, New York, N.Y., 1973.

Johnson, Hugh. **The International Book of Trees,** Mitchell Beazley Publishers, Ltd., London, England, 1973.

Kiaer, Eigil. **Garden Shrubs and Trees in Color,** Illustrated by Vemer Hancke, Blanford Press, London, England, 1965.

Knussmann, Gerd. **Die Baume Europas,** Verlag Paul Parey, Berlin und Hamburg, Germany, 1968.

Kumlein, L.L. **Evergreens,** Rinehart and Co., Inc. New York, N.Y., 1954

Kumlein, L.L. **The Friendly Evergreens,** D. Hill Nursery Co., Dundee, IL., 1946.

Lancaster, Roy. **Trees for Your Garden,** Charles Scribner,s and Sons, New York,N.Y., 1974.

Leathart, Scott. **Trees of the World,** A. & W. Publishers, Inc., New York, N.Y. 1977.

Lemmon, Robert S. **The Best Loved Trees of America,** Doubleday & Co., Garden City, N.Y., 1952.

Kevin Lynch. **Site Planning,** M.I.T. Press, Cambridge, MA., 1962.

Morton Arboretum, Lisle, Illinois. **Bulletin of Popular Information,** various **Bulletins** are of interest in this regard, among these are:
    September-October 1945 - **Know Plant Shapes Before You Plant.**
    June 1944 - **Roadside Planting of Native Illinois Trees and Shrubs.**
    September 1944 - **The Edge of the Forest.**
    April 1946 - **Hawthorn Traits.**

Ministry of Housing and Local Government, **Trees in Town and City,** Her Majesty's Stationery Office, London, England, 1958.

Mitchell, Alan and Michael A. Ruggiero, **Spotter's Guide to Trees of North America,** Mayflower Books, New York, N.Y., 1979.

Peattie, Donald Culross. **The Natural History of Trees,** Houghton-Mifflin Co., New York, N.Y., 1950.

Perard, Victor. **How to Draw,** Pitman Publishing Co., New York, N.Y., 1949.

Petrides, George A. **A Field Guide to Trees and Shrubs,** Houghton-Mifflin Co., Boston, MA. 1958.

Petrides, George A. **A Field Guide to Trees and Shrubs,** Houghton-Mifflin Co., Boston, MA., 1972.

Phillips, Roger. **Trees of North America and Europe,** Random House, New York, N.Y., 1978.

Polunin, Oleg. **Trees and Bushes of Europe,** Oxford University Press, New York, N.Y., 1976.

Ramsey, Charles G. and Harold R. Sleeper. **Architectural Graphic Standards,** John Wiley & Inc., New York, N.Y., 1959.

Rines, Frank M. **Landscape Drawing with Pencil,** Sterling Publishing Co., New York, N.Y., 1964.

Robinson, Florence Bell. **Palette of Plants,** The Garrard Press, Champaign, IL., 1950.

Rogers, Walter E. **Tree Flowers of Forest, Park and Street,** Dover Publications, Inc. New York, N.Y., 1965.

Rushforth, Keith. **The Pocket Guide to Trees,** Simon and Schuster, New York, N.Y., 1981.

Simon and Schuster's. **Guide to Trees,** Simon and Schuster, New York, N.Y., 1977.

Simon and Schuster's **Guide to Trees,** A Firesign Book published by Simon and Schuster, New York, N.Y., 1969.

Smith, Alice Upham. **Trees in the Winter Landscape,** Holt, Rinehart & Winston, New York, 1969.

Smith, Alice Upham. **Trees in the Winter Landscape,** Holt, Rinehart & Winston, New York, N.Y., 1969.

Symonds, George W.D. **The Tree Identification Book,** M. Barrows & Co., New York, N.Y., 1963.

U.S. Department of Agriculture. **Trees,** (Yearbook of Agriculture), U.S. Government Printing Office, Washington, D.C., 1949.

Vedel, Helge and Johan Lange. **Trees and Bushes in Wood and Hedgerow,** Methuen & Co., Ltd., 11 New Fetter Lane, Nondon, England EC4, 1965.

Viertel, Arthur T. **Trees, Shrubs and Vines.** State University College of Forestry at Syracuse University, Syracuse, N.Y., 1961.

Wyman, Donald. **Trees for American Gardens,** The Macmillan Co., New York, N.Y., 1956.

Wyman, Donald. **Shrubs for American Gardens,** The Macmillan Co., New York, N.Y. 1956.

Wyman, Donald. **Trees for American Gardens,** (Second edition), The Macmillan Co., New York, N.Y., 1965.

Zion, Robert L. **Trees for Architecture and the Landscape,** Reinhold Publishing Co., New York, N.Y., 1968.

Zucker, Isabel. **Flowering Shrubs,** D. Van Nostrand Co., Inc. Princeton, N.J., 1966.